Crucial words

Conditions for contemporary architecture
Edited by Gert Wingårdh and Rasmus Wærn

Birkhäuser
Basel · Boston · Berlin

Introduction

Gert Wingårdh
Rasmus Wærn

"I have never loved working for others." This is how Massimiliano Fuksas begins his self-examinatory description of work with his associates in the architects' office. Fuksas, part of the renowned nomenclatura of celebrity architects, is brutally frank about the exacting, unfair conditions that put pressure on both his associates and himself personally. His description of the architect's unremitting labour introduces this collection of *crucial words* for present-day architecture. Thirty answers later, the author Orhan Pamuk rounds off with a description of architecture as experience. Pamuk has written perhaps more than any other author about housing, and when he assembles his experiences dreams become more important than planned reality. *A building's homeliness issues from the dreams of those who live in it.* Between these two poles – the architect's brief but intensive wrestling match with the process, and the people who are to live in the buildings which will, hopefully, outlive their creators – extends everything we call architecture. Both genesis and perception demand their descriptions. There's more to the picture than meets the eye.

To every age its words. Terms which attempt, in a few syllables, to describe intentions which many can agree on but few are able to pin down. Vagueness causes problems, both in the creation of architecture and in the understanding of it. "The obscurely uttered is the obscurely cogitated," in the oft-quoted words of the nineteenth-century Swedish poet Esaias Tegnér. His meaning was clear: the bombastic artificiality of Neo-Romanticism obstructed the clarity which was the true purpose of art. Sincerity and genuine candour alone can point the way to real progress.

In his work, the architect uses more words than pictures. Although many of the words have a decisive bearing on the genesis of architecture, their meaning is often very unclear. There is nothing to be gained from such vagueness. To understand the preconditions of architecture – our own as well as other people's – the key concepts must be brought out for scrutiny. It has not been our ambition to create a reference book that provides unambiguous answers of universal and eternal validity. The authors' reflections on the keywords we have put forward are both subjective and temporary, and for that very reason are especially valid here and now. To shed light on these central concepts we have looked for authors with more than ordinary powers of observation. The mix of words and authors, needless to say, is personal: they point to phenomena and approaches which we also consider important to an understanding of the architecture we create.

Experience, nature and the body are recurrent perspectives in many essays and also in the illustrations we have chosen to elucidate the concepts. A fourth category, which might be termed the practitioner's reflections, centres round the conditions of planning. The political and commercial conditions for present-day architecture are often a more important precondition than the *genus loci*. They are seldom written in letters of fire on the finished building, but are a prerequisite for judging its qualities rightly.

Some texts describe shortcomings of today's architecture, such as atmosphere, memories or desire. Others – such as city branding, globalisation or wheelchairs – focus on the consequences of the new conditions in which architecture has to operate. Many writers draw the same conclusions: tiring of a perpetual hunt for novelty, they plead for the enduring values of architecture. It would be tempting to see in this a trend resembling the last century's disgust with civilisation, which was embraced not only by intellectuals but also by practising architects and planners generally. But this is not the case. Rather it is the gap between ideals and realities which nourishes the frustrating fact that far too much architecture is nowadays concerned with scoring points quickly. At the same time we know that there is always scope for projects with reflection, albeit perhaps on the margin.

How this margin can be widened is an underlying theme in many essays. The text on "landscape" quotes Le Corbusier, who wanted to see Arcadia in all directions. Paradise was to extend in every direction. Corbu's vision lived on under post-modernism, but no further. In today's world, that aspiration seems not just unattainable but also unnecessary. Today a passing dysfunction in places and cities can be seen, not always as a deficiency but instead as an asset. Not everything can or should be ordered and aestheticised. But when marginalised environments are taken well in hand, the disadvantage often presents expressive opportunities of a special kind.

Architecture as built experience provides the theme of many texts. Fragmentation of space may be difficult and sometimes unnecessary to influence, but fragmentation of time can be counteracted in a different way altogether. There is, as Juhani Pallasmaa writes, a quality in the ties between slowness and memory. In despair at having to create housing with no relation whatsoever to anything that had gone before, Orhan Pamuk abruptly curtailed an incipient career as architect. It took him a long time to realise that drawing can also comprehend a living relationship to history. If that experience had been gained earlier, the world would have lost a great author. And possibly gained a great architect.

In the text on "transformation" we read that the big changes in history have seldom come out of processes intended to revolutionise. Call into question, perhaps, but less rarely asseverate. Consequently the great experiences await those who patiently go about reshaping a place, rather than tearing it all down. The book as a whole stresses the close relationship between the future and history. Experience is the foundation on which modern architecture is also fashioned. Even the most unambiguously forward-looking contribution in the whole book – Hans Ulrich Obrist on the future – has to step back a couple of paces in order to extrapolate a trend forwards.

Nature is the most powerful concept ever created for the description of culture. It stands, umbrella-like, over both landscape and organic matter; but body, desire, ornament and the slit also refer to Nature, in various senses. So too, indeed very much so, does ecology, which is present wherever the fateful issues of architecture are pointed out. In an uninhibited attempt to formalise environmental awareness, the term "organic" has come to denote everything from biomorphous blobs to rational organisation charts. There is every reason to relieve the concept of its subsidiary meaning of "quality".

The body's protection is architecture's *raison d'être*. In this way the focus on images of human beings rather than on buildings implies the taking of a stand. Human bodily and spiritual needs as a precondition of present-day architecture are indeed the focal point of several texts. The body is our social representative, but it also represents proportions and ideals. Just as people communicate with the world around them more through their orifices than with their actual body, so does the building. The slit, a reference word in its own right, is described as the *clou* of the mass. The absolute aperture, becoming more and more palpable as it narrows. The gender perspective is inescapable and is definitely among the most crucial. It could have been a reference word in its own right, but instead is now touched on in various texts, not least the one dealing with ornament, describing its shift from the erotic and sacred to compensation for lost beauty.

Some contributions describe the specific preconditions of Nordic and Swedish architecture, such as wheelchairs. Accessibility is a vital task in the conversion of Swedish buildings, but in addition to enabling the mobility-impaired to get in everywhere, this concern should also be capable of generating lasting changes in architecture. In the context of globalised equality, such differences can provide new regional idiosyncrasies, just as post-war housing construction endowed Nordic architecture with an identity of its own.

The reflective practitioner reads and writes. Architecture, both our own and others, requires constant explanation. Conditions in the consumer society of the western world are often strikingly similar. As Carsten Thau writes, the requirement of being attractive does not necessarily mean being glamorous. Accordingly, the conditions in which a Swedish practice has to operate are describable from both an Italian and an American perspective. For all of us, it is a matter of finding oneself in a world of mass culture, in which references and concepts are key notions. If, in times gone by, these were derived from sources remote in time but near in space, the tendency today is to look far off in space but near in time. As a concept this is a logical effect of an internationalised image culture, but architecture does not have to confine itself to creating the expected. This book presents alternatives taken from both the workaday and the festive context.

To those reading this book as a manual, we would like to sum up the authors' experience right away: make buildings affording abundant opportunities for observation. To those reading the book as an attempted apologia for their own ambitions and those of others, we would offer the following cautionary words of Carl Sagan: "Precisely because of human fallibility, extraordinary claims require extraordinary evidence."

Crucial words

Architects
Atmosphere
Body
City Branding
Competitions
Computer
Concept
Corporate
Desire
Doers
Europe
Everyday
Experiment
Formalism
Future
Globalization
Humanism
Landscape
Memory
Modernity
Nature
Nordic
Organic
Ornament
Photography
Slit
Technology
Tradition
Transformation
Wheelchair
Why

Architects

By Massimiliano Fuksas and Elisa Fuksas
Architect, Italy, France and Germany
Architect and filmmaker, Italy

First of all, I have never loved working for others. I have always been under the impression that being young implies a degree of arrogance and always being on the go, not having time for anything. You constantly feel that you have to do everything, immediately, because contrary to how it may seem, being under thirty is no excuse to wait for anything. Waiting is not part of the game, at least not this game.

I have a love-hate relationship with my collaborators, to whom I show both respect and irritation. This is like something you are really enthusiastic about which, once you achieve it, you immediately forget all about. It is an unbalanced and unfair relationship; I am both with and against them. I would like them to read my mind, without doubts in its interpretation and without second thoughts. At the same time, it is the last thing I am thinking about. It is a daily struggle, a war with unforeseeable truces, which of course I cannot allow. We cannot stop, not even for a moment. The mechanism is unstoppable, and whoever is part of it is on a treadmill. The people I work with every day, my closest colleagues, think that I am very hard to please. In actual fact, what I ask of them is simply cleverness, their cleverness. I cannot tolerate stupidity of actions taken in the full knowledge that such actions serve no purpose. I do not tolerate tryouts, temporary solutions, or the long way round to get somewhere. The masses of paper they print as an expression of self-congratulation: as if they needed an outsider to tell them that they have produced a good drawing, a good project, made an effective choice. Or the exact opposite. This is not architecture. Architecture is not about self-congratulation, it is about passion. Everything is in the head and in the eyes, not in finite, rendered images. They are not just fragments of a constantly moving constellation. They serve to communicate, tell a story, but they are not the story itself. What I want is the actual result. Somewhere else. The clarity of a solution which is immediately seen to be the right one, without having to ask others for their opinion. Without consultation. Without complications. Simplicity as evidence of truth. A good idea does not have to be mulled over. In my studio the only true rule is the need to move forward, to have quick reactions. Always to think about tomorrow, the next project, competition, dream. There is no time to chat, discuss and theorise. We must do. Experiment. See.

Academia is a safe world, but far away from the force of creation. From its anarchy. What I want to capture – and what I want them to capture – is the speed and immediacy of thought: the idea must not be filtered. Instead, its brutality and original power must be preserved.

They do not have to add anything, simply cut. Thousands of times I have pondered on a "method" of finding the right people to work with; many architects carry out genuine entrance tests, prepare quasi-official questionnaires and forms. They want to know everything about the candidates, schools, parents, insurance policies, income, right back to their ancestors.

But this is not the way I do things. My problem, and also my strength, is faith: I have always thought that everyone can be better than they think they are. Me included.

Master Mies van der Rohe in the steel tube chair, photo taken by Werner Blaser. See also Axel Sowa's text on the body, page 18. Copyright Werner Blaser.

Atmosphere

By Falk Jaeger
Professor of Theory of Architecture at Dresden
University of Technology, Germany

"From pure function comes abstract beauty," exclaimed Erich Mendelsohn in 1924, not entirely enthusiastically, when faced with gigantic corn silos in Chicago with their "awkward, childlike forms, full of natural power, surrendered to pure need". He highlighted a dilemma that modernism, which was evolving at that time, faced from the beginning and continues to this day. Abstract beauty is a noble aim, which nevertheless seems to be incompatible with humankind's basic needs for atmosphere and security. Average citizens can no longer endure the lofty heights of the aesthetic sphere. They demand sentimental values, cosiness, and even comfort (which experts prefer to call "charm"). Ever since, architects have encountered this dilemma again and again and have tried to solve it. Adolf Loos, who believed ornament to be a waste of effort, at least gave his clients blazing marble and interestingly grained wooden surfaces to feast their eyes upon. Bruno Taut spiritedly resorted to coloured paint and Le Corbusier became ever more baroque in his later works.

There are still architects who would prefer a world they could furnish with building manifestos and soulless housing. Many are students of Oswald Mathias Ungers, the exponent of "architecture as science", who turned many a house into an uninhabitable work of art, into a perfect artefact radiating spatial coldness.

There are not even idealistic proportions such as the golden section or Fibonacci series, nor the metric, Euclidean space, which would stimulate people. What modernism lacks is topological space with human interactions and an atmosphere that speaks to all the senses. This means an acoustic atmosphere. An atmosphere of light and colour. An atmosphere of materials with their haptic, sensual qualities, which encourage us to touch and feel.

The advanced field of light composition, as mastered by Le Corbusier and Paul Rudolph, has gone out of fashion. And what Leon Battista Alberti propagated in the fifteenth century, namely that light and shadows can spiritually change space, is still compelling.

Architecture, even that of the perfectionists of modernism, feels cold and sterile and is often deadly boring. Their works do not lack "noble beauty", but they remain "without interest" as described by Kant in his *Critique of the Power of Judgement*. Detail and finish are refined to the highest perfection, but even significant structures only rarely succeed in generating emotive spaces and comforting atmospheres. Meanwhile, others have no qualms about helplessly reviving grandmother's flowery wallpaper and grandfather's wing chair,

because they are unable to overcome the deficit in any other way. "Architecture arouses sentiments. The architect's task, therefore, is to make these sentiments more precise," proposed Adolf Loos in 1925. His advice has been forgotten.

It lies in the soulless perfection of industrial production of aluminium windows, glass doors and steel furniture. It lies in the computerised, serial design methods, which offer standard solutions as a rapid answer and thus do not exactly hinder individual ideas, but do not trigger them either. Only a few architects initially build working models to check the proportions, spatial effects and incidences of light of their designs. Many leave the task of creating an atmosphere to the construction company or the users themselves. Atmosphere is the most powerful factor in experiencing architecture, and therefore also in forming an overall assessment, because it touches upon feelings and emotions. However, this factor is ignored or only used unknowingly by most architects. Generating atmospheres has a lot to do with the theatre, with the knowledge of directorial effects of light, colours and materials – in the eyes of many architects a frivolous career.

Nonetheless, during the founding of modernism, there were theoreticians like the herald of glass architecture Paul Scheerbart, who, in 1914, while tirelessly arguing on emotional levels, advocated glass architecture filled with colourful light, because of its atmospheric qualities.

Abstinence disguised as respectability is based on a dread of emotionality, which has always been accompanied by strong colours. Colours belong to those feelings, which everyone is ready to experience spontaneously and decisively. Whoever builds with colour exposes himself to spirited, at times unrestrained, criticism. Additionally, every person reacts differently to colours and surprising spatial creations. You can never please everyone. As long as architects direct their attention exclusively to the observation of functional and economical constraints or bloodless studies on architectural theory, or else erect spectacular architectural sensations, without really worrying about the wishes and needs of the user, acceptance of modern contemporary architecture among the wider population will remain low.

Bill Viola. The Messenger, 1996. Video/sound installation. Photo: Kira Perov.

Body

By Axel Sowa
Editor-in-chief of *l'architecture d'aujourd'hui*, France

We do not know what the body is *in itself*. What is certain is that as long as it is healthy and functional it can be lived in easily. Yet in most cases the body remains hidden from its user. In the dark of the moment that has been lived, the body itself hardly manifests itself. Direct physical existence only becomes a puzzle when you start analysing it. You can bring the body to life with the aid of cameras, scanners or X-ray machines. Yet in the end all these aids actually remove us from the body. Probing, dissecting and analytical questioning cut through the impenetrable self-evidence of the body. Communicable knowledge of the body can only be expected at a distance from the body. In order to get it to speak, interpret it, understand it, impart its concept, we use systems of symbols, e.g. anatomical diagrams or ergonomic graphs. These symbol systems socialising the body presuppose agreement, convention, typification and coding, which in turn becomes an abstraction, a symbol for something else. The functionalised body of the worker, the seductive body of the advertisement, the emaciated body of the drought victim, become models, ciphers of mass communication. "By and large," says Jean-Luc Nancy, "we only know and understand the typical body, we can only imagine it that way. The body, where it is irrelevant whether it is *here*, whether it is the *here* or *there* of a place, and where it is much more important that it acts as the steward or curator of a sense". (1.)

Moreover, the body is always coded in terms of its possible applicative links. In recent architectural representations, the anthropomorphic bag figures were replaced by images of dynamic sporting contemporaries. The photo-realistic image of the body of anonymous users, consumers or passers-by is incorporated into the architectural drawing to demonstrate that the satisfaction of the "average human being" is taken into consideration in the projected environment. As Hans Belting has shown, there is a close link between the body image and the human image. (2.) The body images which have also represented the corresponding human images are as changeable as that which, in the course of history, has been understood as the "human being". The body images have represented the incarnation of God (the Gospels), the ideal proportions of a cosmic harmony (Leonardo da Vinci), the presence of Shaman power (voodoo cult), the statistical mean value (Ernst Neufert) or the potential "designability" of the self (Cindy Sherman).

In February 1984 the journal *l'architecture d'aujourd'hui* published a monograph devoted to the work of Jean Nouvel, modest at that time. (3.) Photographs were published together with an interview with the architect, which show Nouvel in various poses: Nouvel in bed with his favourite read, Nouvel in thought, or Nouvel vested with the attributes of a producer or critic. Here the image of the architect's body is used playfully as a means of social interaction and accompanies the interview text. The body of the architect is given the opportunity to enter the media and is stage-managed, clothed and arranged especially for this purpose. In hindsight, Nouvel turns out to be a visionary. Representations of the bodies of architects can now be found in the advertising for building components, in brochures announcing congresses, on the title pages of Spanish specialist journals, and wherever the architectural spectacle creates such a stir that a public, no matter how indifferent, can no longer escape it. The almost unlimited possibility of duplication of body images is used not only by film stars but also by all architects who want to make their mark. The omnipresence of their images not only attracts attention but also projects a semblance of intimacy. But what is the purpose of this obtrusive approach of Jean, Jacques, Zaha, Norman, Massimiliano, Frank and Daniel? What purpose is served by the permanent photographic presence of people whom we never see in everyday life? What is their significance?

Our present star system is definitely a body problem. Individual bodies make their presence felt. They stand out from the closed corpus of their professional status. Through the media machine they are repelled by the hardness of prosaic everyday life. Released from the disciplinary limits of their corporation they enter into the orbit of spatial ubiquity. However, the impatience of the stars who still want to win fame before their death is as old as the profession of architecture itself. The mediatisation of the architect's body is not a new phenomenon. It appears early on in the writings and treatises of the Renaissance architects who wanted to establish their career as independent artists. In a historical outline Laurent Baridon showed that Jean Goujon or Philibert de l'Orme played to the gallery in the frontispiece of their published works. (4.) By taking up the *topos* of the Dinocrates figure justified by Vitruvius, says Baridon, the architects lay claim to social and technical power.

In this case the body image has at least two components. First, it announces the physical, unique existence of the author, who is served by his or her self-portrait as a token of his or her work. At the same time the individual body is also a constituent of a social body, a new learned profession which is released from the bonds of the craft guilds and therefore relies upon confidence-building measures. Here the body image establishes the link between work, personality and professional ethos. It is the medium for justifying individual and professional reputation. The first body images published and circulated by the architects of the Renaissance serve to protect a proposed programme. They form the basis of a new discipline. The calculation has been done: the most important representatives of the profession were then granted access to royal houses and academies.

Until the end of the nineteenth century, the reproduction of body images, busts and portraits of architects remain bound by the disciplinary limits of the profession. For centuries the individual architect's body has been provided with the tools of his or her trade - the circle, the rolled-up plan or the model, for the purposes of representation. The forms of the representation did not change until the second half of the nineteenth century. Since the advent of new consumer behaviour, simulated by illustrated journals and by the specialist trade in fashion and luxury, bodies have been under pressure. They must still be based on models, but these models change from one season to the next. Physical appearance is no longer a misfortune. It becomes the object of conscious, individual choice. A new type of self-production is created with the figure of the dandy. The dandy, who through striking clothing and behaviour makes clear that he places no particular value on social respect, provokes the bourgeoisie to reject him, and manoeuvres himself into *splendid isolation*. Through crazy stylisations for the production of extemporaneity and independence, the body is now brought into play by criticizing established norms. (5.)

Initially the architects followed the model of Baudelaire, the "flaneurs" and absinth drinkers only timidly and to this extent their appearance no longer needed follow corporative rules. The image of the body - such as that of Mackintosh or Morris - could be freely selected, and now served to represent the *persona* of the creator. The individualisation of the pose and of outward appearance opened up a new game with expectations and customer requirements. As bourgeois rituals and accepted truths faded in time, the architect could no longer satisfy a constant demand. He had to risk the new and play the role of the avant-gardist. In demonstrative freedom from tension the architect showed that he is not impressed by the new. Like the lookout for a reconnaissance party, he first looked at what is new and then created it himself. The protagonists of the so-called heroic

moderns used their physical presence in this sense. Mies van der Rohe or Le Corbusier commissioned photographs to circulate their body images. The legendary photograph by Werner Blaser shows the elegantly clothed body of Mies. In a calm and relaxed pose in which he is leaning back, Mies carries out the load test on his seat of steel tube, whose material stress resists the weight of the master. Lucien Hervé depicts Le Corbusier in front of his *Unité d'habitation* in Marseille. The hand of the architect touches the concrete wall of the building, his arm showing a sharp shadow over the wall relief of the Modulor figure. The architect takes as his formal basis the human figure of the Modulor he designed. Whilst Corbu propagates the general reliability of his work with the Modulor, the image simultaneously announces the dimensionless claim of the architect who poses as the author of a new human image. These examples show that self-production followed new rules which emphasised in particular the unique relationship between the human being and his work. Parallel to the work, the body of the architects becomes a problem of self-design. In order not to appear arbitrary the attributes of self-production (spectacles, hat, bow tie, shawl or cigar), once chosen, must be resolutely re-used. The freely discovered mask which conceals the human body must be as invariable, resistant and dependable as that body. Although the public actor may appear as a rebel, clown, *lonely hero or outlaw*, he must remain true to his costume.

The ritual reuse of the same poses and their multiplication in the media are, in the end, indispensable in the present day. The most exposed protagonists of the international architectural spectacle could not assert themselves without the images of their bodies. The body as an art form must not miss its entrance. The penetrating repetition and continuous presence of the same bodies take place against the background of a general, in most cases invisible precariousness. Today, architecture has become a difficult business. The overwhelming majority of European architects work on the edge of poverty and survive in single-person offices. Their order volume is shrinking because architectural offices are being increasingly drained of planning skills. They are to be found in the development departments of business banks with large real estate portfolios, in logistics and the maintenance and consulting sector, in facility management or in rendering and visualisation agencies. Most of today's construction process is prepared by anonymous planners and is largely determined by legal, economic, industrial and logistic parameters. The field of architecture, which is still covered and illustrated by journals and magazines, is very varied. A German journal commented on this: "At present the international debate on architecture appears to be characterised by a unique uncertainty. All the formal trends of the last few years have asserted themselves and have therefore become superfluous". (6.)

The body of the architect has not yet become superfluous. It appears to be the last nail that is holding together lifeworks that are drifting apart. The body is the last authentic authority expected to show any sort of continuity. Whilst our ingenious creators concern themselves in different ways about dematerialisation, folding, blobs, ornaments, graphs and context references, their bodies remain what they always were: fat or thin, agile or tired, bald or hairy. Some architects have already recognised that their bodies are subject to the compulsion to be constantly visible. Where they cannot be present in person, they must arrange for their bodies to be transmitted directly by video conference. Only through the *staccato* of the appearances, micro-events, and only through breathtaking speed can attention still be held and auditoria filled. The most famous occupants of the star carousel are circling the earth faster than the journalists can follow them. The athletic performance of the architects' bodies is now also celebrated in so-called marathon events. This first happened at the London Serpentine Gallery and more recently also during the Kassel documenta. In an eight-hour session on 5 August, Rem Koolhaas and Hans Ulrich Obrist asked more than twenty artists, architects, historians, urbanists and journalists about their work and world views. (7.) In breathtaking continuous presence, Obrist and Koolhaas, suffering from jetlag, resisted purely physically the divergence of contents, replies, attitudes, and earned our greatest respect for doing so.

After prolonged development, the body of the architect is no longer an indication of nationality or faithfulness to the original. The body is no longer part of a larger, social body. The body no longer appears in avant-garde associations either, but still only without bonds - in the singular. Neither beautiful characteristics, nor attributes, poses or clothes, are of any actual significance. The only value worthy of attention stems from its omnipresence, which relies on medium circulation and communication. Yet what is the deeper meaning of the omnipresent, globally available images of architects' bodies? They are magi with which we have no dialogue. We cannot even say with certainty what they stand for. Perhaps they exist only to conceal something. What might that be? Architecture perhaps?

1. Jean-Luc Nancy, Corpus, Paris, 2000, quoted from the German translation, Berlin, 2003, p. 61.
2. For this see: "The body image as a human image, a representation in crisis", in Hans Belting, Bild-Anthropologie (Image Anthropology), Munich, 2001.
3. L'Architecture d'aujourd'hui (The Architecture of Today), No. 231, "Jean Nouvel 1977–83", Paris, February 1984, p. 3 ff.
4. Lecture by Laurent Baridon at the international colloquium "The Founding Myths of Architecture", Valetta, Malta, 7–9 October 2005. See also: Le mythe de Dinocrate: L'architecte, le corps et l'utopie (The Myth of Dinocrates: The Architect, the Body and Utopia), 2008.
5. See: "Das Verschwinden des Dandys" (The Disappearance of the Dandy), in Beat Wyss, Die Wiederkehr des Neuen (The Recurrence of the New), Hamburg, 2007, p. 200 ff.
6. Newsletter from archplus, 31 July 2007, on Mini-Marathon-Germany,
documenta 12, Kassel, documenta magazines, Archplus, Mini-Marathon-Germany
7. Video clips at: www.archplus.net.

Giorgio De Chirico. Self-portrait with a rose, 1923. Copyright De Chirico/BUS 2007.

City Branding

By Janet Ward
Associate Professor of History
at the University of Nevada, USA

City branding – understood as the focusing of our psychologically rooted images of cities toward cultural-capitalist gains – is being used to regenerate cities at a seemingly ever accelerating rate. Not surprisingly, architecture is playing a key role in this urban sleight of hand. The cultural turn for cities (nowadays expressed in terms of iconic architecture by the likes of Daniel Libeskind or Frank Gehry rather than in any actual cultural collections or content) can be easily applied to cities able to afford that particular transformation.

Nowhere is the branding process more blatantly visible than in Las Vegas. When even Studio Daniel Libeskind has been hired to design a shopping mall for the casino industry's capital – a massive, fragmented, star-shaped cluster right in the middle of MGM Mirage's new high-rise CityCenter adjoining the Strip – we have to admit that architecture's relationship to boosterism for the contemporary city has been reconfigured. As Libeskind himself has stated, his corporate clients, like MGM Mirage with its seven billion dollar Project CityCenter, have been embracing his bold dramatic forms far more willingly than his non-corporate customers (Libeskind, 2007). In other words, where until recently a museum designed by a signature architect was a prerequisite for a city's image-makeover, by means of a covertly commercial site of high culture (the so-called "Bilbao effect"), today that same star architectural turn and concomitant boosterist success for the city can be seamlessly applied to more openly commercial sites. The cultural character of a city can thus be fed and fêted even without the originating sites of high culture.

Las Vegas has the ability to draw up to 40 million tourists per year, and has benefited enormously from the hugely successful advertising campaign (by communications agency R&R Partners in 2005) that rebranded it as a *sexy* – as opposed to a *seedy* – Sin City: "What happens here, stays here." Yet the city's now global tagline, one that implies a resort for individualistic and sensual freedom rather than just a lowest common denominator tourist destination, is but part of an ongoing refinement process, one that is leading the city out of its former "fear and loathing" epithet of potential moral and financial bankruptcy (itself an *Ur*-fear of the modern urban condition). The blending of architectural techniques that service both mass consumerism and high culture has rendered much of Las Vegas's appeal at once more innocuous, gentrified, and representative. The city's extravagant echelon climbing is being expressed most clearly in terms of its real estate, specifically via the high densification of the area in and immediately around the Strip, of which the condos and retail district of Project CityCenter, scheduled to open in 2009, form a significant part. A new urban core, with landmark architectural imports by the likes of Helmut Jahn and Foster and Partners, and with financing led by the world's leading casino corporation, is being forged to re-anchor the already multifaceted Strip experience. And so this is where Libeskind's luxury mall will literally become the CityCenter's and potentially the entire Las Vegas valley's new nucleus. Of course, the irony is that, in tandem with the rest of the high-end Strip, this future CityCenter is not even located on land that is incorporated by the actual *city* of Las Vegas. But no matter: here we are witnessing city branding, and a constant rebuttressing or rebranding of the city's set of images into new versions that destabilize the old, in its most powerful form. Our product, Las Vegas, is on the move.

The above example is but one in a broad evolution of and by cities toward a competitive realm of the virtual-cum-architectural, in which image-city competes against image-city (both of other cities and of previous, less desirable incarnations of themselves). Geographer David Harvey has defined this as a shift toward "urban entrepreneurialism," a distinguishing feature of the service economy in the post-Fordist, essentially post-1970s era (Harvey, 2000). This trend, a spin-off of globalization, has co-opted even socialist urban governments, forcing them to behave like neo-conservatives and engage in inter-urban, competitive city-marketing, usually with an investment focus on the regeneration of the downtown through heritage tourism, infrastructural upgrades (in rail, air, highway, and telecommunications), and the endless reproduction of certain urban structures shown to be highly effective in staging spectacular ephemera – such as convention centers, hotels, stadiums, museums, and, yes, malls, preferably by top signature architects. Harvey refuses to totally demonize the ongoing hegemony of urban entrepreneurialism, stressing that its most frequent crime, namely a "triumph of image over substance," remains a relatively innocuous house of cards. Moreover, as Harvey implies, the creation of a positive boosterist image for a city can go a long way toward forging solidarity: in short, a renewed identity for its denizens. Here Harvey goes some way toward the more radical approach taken by Rem Koolhaas that, quite simply, there is no more escaping the rules of marketability for urban development: the architecture of shopping and the architecture of tourism are now viewed as synonymous with a city's sense of place (Koolhaas, 2000).

Therefore even *civitas* can be the unlikely outcome of such an obviously artificial production line as postmodern urban boosterism, on condition that it is performed well. We can refer to the title of the German edition of an essay collection by urbanist Mike Davis, who makes the case against *Casino Zombies* (Davis, 1999). We may well ask: is the fate of totally branded, commercialized cities that of casino-cultural zombification? Should we mourn the loss of a yearning for an originating, organically grown urban essence: the *agora*? Or can we approach the matter of today's urban realities in a less over-defensive, atrophied way?

Davis, Mike (1999), Casino Zombies und andere Fabeln aus dem Neon-Westen der USA, trans. Steffen Emrich and Britta Grell. Berlin: Schwarze Risse.
Harvey, David (2000), 'From Managerialism to Entrepreneurialism: The Transformation in Urban Governance in Late Capitalism', in The City Cultures Reader, ed. Malcolm Miles, Tim Hall and Iain Borden. New York: Routledge. Orig. 1989, in Geografiska Annaler 71.1: 3–18.
Koolhaas, Rem (2000), "Shopping. Harvard Project on the City," in Koolhaas, Stefano Boeri, and Sanford Kwinter, eds. Mutations. Bordeaux: ACTAR.
Libeskind, Daniel (July 2007). Keynote discussion at the "InEvidence" urbanism conference, University of Cambridge, Cambridge.

Competitions

By Wilfried Wang
Architect, Germany, Professor of Architecture
at the University of Texas, USA

Architectural competitions have their modern origin in the formation of professional bodies such as chambers of architects. In the true Enlightenment sense, competitions became ways by which, until recently, architects defined their worth in society. Trust was placed in the ability of the profession's peers to select the work that best suited a site and program.

In contrast to other fields, competitions in architecture were not considered to be means of establishing dominance of one architect over another, but of ensuring that the best building would be realized for the immediate benefit of the commissioning body and the benefit of society at large. Architectural competitions were held not so much for the "survival" of the fittest, but for the realization of the fittest, the notion of fitness here also being used in the sense of the suitability and appropriateness of a piece of architecture in order to sustain that part of civilization.

The holding of a competition in this spirit required a client organization to understand the necessity for excellence in design above other issues such as short-term financial gain (be it as a result of the advantage taken by realizing a design solution that appears to be suitable for a brief period, by using cheaper materials that have a short life expectation, by adopting a typological solution that is less receptive for future demands, by giving preference to a more tried and tested option that fails to maintain levels of admiration and respect or that simply does not inspire people, etc.). It required the selection of a jury able to discern good from bad, appropriate from inappropriate, innovative from conventional.

Competitions in architecture required a form of social solidarity within the profession that accepted the wisdom of client organizations and the intelligence of juries. It required a submission to rules and regulations that allowed for a competition entry to be judged on the basis of its intrinsic value, that is, without regard to the jury's knowledge of the author of a design.

It presupposed that competing architects would act responsibly in relation to the interests not only of the client, but also of civil society, thus encompassing issues of communal symbolism, efficacy, financial prudence, fitness vis-à-vis the immediate and larger contexts. Further, competitions in architecture required an interested and informed public that would be presented with results by a variety of media via reporters who at least in part described the designs with a sense of respect and objectivity while also providing a personal assessment.

Architectural competitions, during the period when they were open and anonymous, were a locus of critical discourse. They were about ideas and values. As such, they were utterly distinct from competitions in other fields of manufacturing and service industries, where there the product to be offered is defined in terms of its form and quality. These largely anonymous architectural competitions were generally open to architects registered in specific regions (whether nations, regions or states). Thus, the regional restriction defined a regional culture and a known dimension of potentially participating architects.

The demise of the Enlightenment form of architectural competition began in the early twentieth century with the rise in the importance of the two-dimensional representation of architecture. In some senses, the requirement to present contextual models at a scale of 1:500 encouraged the simplistic representation of architectural form in order to ensure an eidetic quality that would ensure the memorability of a competition entry. During the second half of the twentieth century, architectural competitions became systematized. Both image and small model (often made of materials that bore no relation to reality) began to lead a discourse of their own. They attained shorthand character quite distinct from the resultant buildings. Members of the competition jury would misread qualities into these forms of presentations. The frequently observed requirement by the professional bodies for there to be a majority of architects within the jury led some clients to believe that they were being overwhelmed by architects' interests.

Towards the end of the twentieth century, when regional restriction was prohibited by international competition regulations (a direct form of globalization) a number of public competitions resulted in a large number of submissions, inundating the technical and design juries, causing large costs to be incurred in the handling of the judging process as well as resulting in exhaustive jury sessions.

The constant reduction in the number of open and anonymous architectural competitions went hand in hand with even larger numbers of entrants. As a result, most commissioners of competitions chose to adopt other forms of competitions, principally to control the numbers of entries: staged competitions with simple submissions at the first stage; pre-qualification methods; lottery systems coupled with direct invitations; direct invitations only; interview selections; just to name some of the alternatives.

While the architectural profession has been forcibly defined as just another "service" industry in conformity with other service industries (with the exception of the legal, medical, health and social welfare professions; and banking and insurance industries), architectural competitions have been absorbed into the legal framework of services competitions as defined by the World Trade Organization, (General Agreement on Trade in Services - GATS) and the European Union's Directive on Services. The architectural profession has generally submitted to this legal framework with the result that, since the twenty-first century, architectural competitions are generally non-anonymous, multi-phased, pre-selected, and/or by invitation.

Thus, the original spirit of architectural competitions has been successfully compromised by "alternative" selection procedures. Furthermore, where clear rules exist for government agencies to run open competitions, endeavors are often made to circumvent such requirements by, for example, establishing so-called public private partnerships that would then be freed from the onus to run competitions at all, or worse, the call for "turnkey" or "design/build" development services, where a building is erected for a fixed sum. Such evident malpractice rarely finds legal action on behalf of either professional bodies or individual architects.

The most pernicious aspect of contemporary forms of architectural competitions, however, is the process of pre-selection. Criteria are established that ensure a screening of potential competitors. These criteria include the testing of the financial background of an architectural office (though in contravention of the EU Directive on Services, §66), computer hardware and software used, number of full-time employees, track-record vis-à-vis the building type under competitive consideration. To outsiders, these screens may appear reasonable. However, neither are such hurdles used in other cultural fields, nor did their absence prevent less experienced architects from submitting worthy designs in the past. The direct consequences of the European Union Directive on Services on architecture is to diminish cultural diversity and most importantly architectural quality as a result of the many discriminatory and circumventive but legal measures taken where previously open and anonymous architectural competitions were held.

Besides the behemoths of the GATS and the European Union, it is the intellectual corruption of the contemporary entertainment industry, of which the two-dimensional representations of buildings are a subservient part, which prevents real architectural competitions from regaining their importance. As long as the economic gain from the editorial exposure of a "spectacular" piece of "architecture" is greater than the cost of placing advertisements in different media, commissioning bodies will continue to seek the faster return on their investment with the aim of establishing an eidetic "brand" with ever more curious images of so-called architecture.

The final eclipse of the conventional open and anonymous architectural competition was therefore brought about by the importation of the nomenclatura or star system into the realm of architecture by the mass media. Instant gratification on investment through "landmarks" by "star architects" has a debilitating effect despite the underlying awareness that this does not lead to architectural quality. However, for the individual corporate client, the fact that established architects have been chosen to participate in a limited, non-anonymous competition guarantees that one way or another a well-known architect will be selected. More often than not, the name and its owner's reputation are more important to such a client than the actual quality of the design, especially when the client has little sense or appreciation for architecture.

As long as the image is more important than the building, as long as the name of the architect automatically stands for "quality" for some clients, there will not be an interest in the return to open and anonymous architectural competitions. Western societies have crossed a Rubicon on this issue; with this they have set a lamentable example to other countries. The exclusion of the architectural profession from the European Union Directive on Services is unlikely. The professional bodies have amply documented their willingness to compromise on a central issue that cannot suffer compromise. Thus, today, when a selection process in the field of architecture bears the label "competition", it generally involves anything but a competition for ideas.

Hilde de Haan and Ids Haagsma, Architects in Competition: International Architectural Competitions of the Last Two Hundred Years, New York 1988.
Cees de Jong and Erik Mattie, Architekturwettbewerbe 1792–1949, Cologne, 1994.
European Union Directive on Services, eur-lex.europa.eu

Trees in Sardinia, shaped by competition with the wind. A form made possible only by the invisible structure underneath, which stretches out without considerations or compulsions. Photographer unknown.

Computer

By Jaime Salazar Rückauer
Architect and editor, Spain and Germany

Few performances are designed as quickly and last as long as architecture. Look around you: some products need years of investigation before they can be produced and reach the consumer. Once produced, they serve us for short periods of time before being replaced by others that are considered to be better. By contrast, a building is normally conceived in weeks, designed in months and produced in one or two years; and used, in most cases, for many decades. In this respect, buildings should be considered as a masterpiece of sustainable production.

At the same time, architectural debates still focus almost exclusively on design, and only marginally on real performance: the life and the use of buildings. Of course, the design of buildings and the architects who conceive them are a substantial aspect of building production. But buildings have a considerable life expectancy. Once built, they are exposed to physical changes and corresponding costs. If we compare buildings to living organisms, they are among the most ancient products of technological creation. Buildings are big, sometimes very big, often rudimentary and imprecise. When compared to other technologies, they slowly add layers of use to their built substance. Moreover, the longevity of buildings – including those which employ the most advanced technology – means that they fall into technical obsolescence. Existing buildings are therefore increasingly perceived as an acute economical problem.

Since the beginning of the computer age, man-made technology has shifted from the inert matter of the mechanized age towards matter that reacts to the effects of time. As soon as a machine was able to process information, its performance over time – rather than its initial conditions – began to play a significant role. This "time" has very little to do with the time of space perception, the so-called fourth dimension of modern architecture besides the three dimensions of space. In relation to architecture, the "time" of the computer age corresponds to the performance time of a building once it has been built. In relation to machines, the "performance time" of architecture cannot yet be considered to be "life" or life-like behaviour, but it does tend, slowly but reliably, to acquire such attributes.

Maybe buildings are not – and will never again be – the highlights of technical evolution, but they are being increasingly assisted by information processing technology during the course of their life, like most products around us. Scepticism towards smart architecture and intelligent environments will therefore be as ephemeral as the flop of the first e-economy. It is a question of time and of processing capacity. In a world that aspires to efficiency, inert machines seem to be inadequate, because they are non-ecological.

If there is a real breakthrough of the computer age in relation to artificial matter, this is it. Since the second half of the twentieth century, man-made artefacts have been increasingly able to process information. This development was initially confined to information processing machines, but today it applies to almost every machine and every environment. Although the physical limits of this evolution are apparent, and have already been predicted, this change is comparable to the industrial revolution that took place over a century ago. After leaving behind its origins, humankind is now returning to them – by creating a manufactured copy.

Concept

By Ingerid Helsing Almaas
Editor-in-chief of *Byggekunst*, Norway

Most architectural projects are based on some kind of underlying idea, often called a "concept". "You must develop a strong concept," tutors in architecture schools repeatedly demand. Architects compliment each other on projects and buildings that are "conceptually coherent", you will even find the word used as an adjective: we will say to an architect that his or her work "is very conceptual". Nonetheless, the word "concept" does not appear in the *Penguin Dictionary of Architecture*, nor will you find it in the indexes of the many reference works by authors like Banister Fletcher, Frampton, Pevsner or Jencks, where you might expect the word to appear, somewhere between "computer" and "concrete". In fact, I cannot remember anyone ever explaining to me exactly what an "architectural concept" is. It is one of those words in our professional language, that has gained meaning by its ubiquity, like "project" or "idea"; it seems indispensable to professional discourse both at a practical and theoretical level, but in fact it covers very different ground for different people.

A practical test

As a test, I recently sent a number of my Norwegian colleagues an e-mail with the obvious question: "What is an architectonic concept?" After only a couple of days I had received over fifty replies. Below are some of them:

"A form that gives the intuitively right answer to a given problem."
"A formal idea that can be realised in practice."
"A basic idea which forms the starting point for the development of form."
"An overall gesture that carries through the entire process from initial sketches to the final project."
"A kind of architectonic DNA, an idea which can be expressed in words as well as in a drawing or a model."
"A navigational tool for the design of architectonic solutions."
"A meeting of heaven and earth."

There were many more, but all these replies confirmed my suspicion that the word is taken to mean a number of different things. But I made some interesting general observations:
 Many people describe a "concept" as something that has a *guiding* function.

Many people see it as a requirement that the concept can be visualised in a simple sketch or diagram. Some also mention a model, although "conceptual models" are probably a rarity in most architects' offices.

People variously think that a concept is an initial and intuitively correct reaction to a problem, which remains static throughout the design process, or that it is something that is tested and adjusted along the way.

Some people describe a concept as something necessary to explain or communicate a project to others, and some people even think this it its main function.

A few people think "concept" is an unnecessary word, its ubiquity dictated entirely by fashion.

It is also interesting to note that it did not take people more than a day or two to get back to me with their responses. "Concept" is obviously a familiar word, in everyday use within the profession, and people had no hesitation in formulating what they thought it meant. So if people are using it as if they know it, perhaps it does not matter if the meanings we give it are different? We all know more or less what we mean and what we are trying to achieve within the architectural profession, and words are, after all, only a means to the final end, the finished building.

The risks of inconsistency

Inconsistency does perhaps create a risk. However, the most important use of language for an architect is not communication with other architects, which often consists of lines, pictures, vague grunts of approval or disapproval and other non-verbal gestures; the most important use of language in architecture is in the communication with our partners and collaborators in the design and construction process. Language is necessary to convince clients, consultants, authorities and the general public that a proposal is sensible and worth paying for. And in this communication, the diversity of meanings attached to pivotal words like "concept" suddenly become very problematic. Clearly, we need to tune this word, "concept"; and for the sake of our professional reputation we need to be more consistent when we use it.

Dictionary definition

The dictionary definition of the word "concept" refers of course to the Latin, and gives the meaning "idea", "general notion" or "invention". It is closely related to the verb "conceive", derived from the Latin prefix *com*, meaning with or together, and *cipere or capere*, meaning to take, or grasp. A strict interpretation of this would be that a "concept" is something that can be grasped by thought. It is also interesting that the word "capable" has the same root, as does the word "captain" – as demonstrated by my respondents who thought that the main function of the architectonic concept was to *guide*. In fact, this idea of guidance seems to separate my respondents roughly into two groups: those who feel that a concept has something to do with architectonic form, and those who do not give it formal connotations.

Concept = form?

All architects faced with a modern, complex building task, like a hospital, a school or an office complex, will know that you cannot develop a building from a given *form*. To be sure, you can work *towards* a certain pre-determined form, but it is doubtful whether this is a productive way of working. If you have a set form or formal ideal you are trying to realise, the changes to the programme, financing and other conditions that inevitably arise during the design and realisation of a building can only cause frustration, and can only be solved through compromise, to the detriment of the very form you were trying to realise. A concept, consequently, is not a form.

A basis for decisions

Many of my respondents, however, described "concept" not as a particular form or set of forms but for better or worse as something you work from, a basis for the development and the detailing of a project:

"An architectonic concept is a set of ground rules that govern all choices through the design process."
"An architectonic concept is a collection of words meant to justify strange angles and shiny things in a project."
"It is a basic thought, which aids or informs the many choices that need to be made in a project."

A simple test: Architects inevitably think that the answer to any question is to build, but it may be that the answer to a given problem is not to build anything at all. And if your basic premise is that a concept is a physical form, *not* building is no longer an option, thereby limiting the number of possible answers. This is an extreme case, perhaps, but telling nonetheless. The idea of an architectonic concept as something that guides your choices, then, is ultimately a more productive definition: that an architectonic concept is something that gives you a basis for making decisions. How do I know whether to use brick or concrete in a building? It can be a purely practical or financial decision, but it can also be the outcome of a basic sequence of ideas, i.e. the architectonic concept. Is it important, for example, to blend into a given physical setting, or to create a contrast? And if we choose a contrast, does brick or concrete do the best job? It is equally important to ask, why a contrast? *Why* is a vital question in the development of an architectonic concept. In fact, you could say that the main function of an architectonic concept is to answer the question *why*. *Why* was it important for Le Corbusier to create a contrast to the landscape in the Villa Savoye? Le Corbusier is one of the few architects who has always expressed his intentions with a project very convincingly, but you can ask the same question, *why*, of any architectural project, and each time you will get a little closer to its conceptual point of departure.

Why?

Why. Form cannot provide an answer. Why did Henry Hoare want to dam a valley in the middle of eighteenth-century England? Well, he wanted to create paradise on earth. Stourhead landscape park is an eighteenth-century vision of Elysium. And when you know what you want, you can ask of any idea that comes into your head, of any decision you face throughout the execution of the project: How does this detail help me create paradise on earth? Where should I plant the trees, what trees should I plant, where should the pavilions be located? And then, of course, those questions have to be answered, which is not always easy. For what is paradise? How is it organised? What does it look like? And what is earth? Because a concept does not *provide* knowledge: a useful architectural concept *activates* knowledge.

A concept cannot be a pre-determined form

An architectural concept is a formless structure of thoughts, which can be described with a few words or a sketch. Architectural form, by contrast, is described in dimensional plans, sections and elevations. The contrary is not possible: You cannot draw an accurate section through a concept, and a diagram cannot be an accurate representation of a form. It is essential to keep these two pivotal terms of architecture distinct from each other: concept is not form. Form is not concept. If you accept, then, that an architectonic concept is a set of ideas that form the basis for decision-making in a project, a concept does not appear through the lightning bolt of individual genius. It is something that can evolve through a long process, with contributions from many people along the way. The latter is particularly important: Rather than belonging to the mysterious realm of inspiration, an architectonic concept becomes a meeting place for the many people involved in the realisation of a complex building: it becomes a common story, a shared aim. The concept for a project can be discussed before a line is drawn on paper. "What are we trying to do?" "We are trying to build paradise on earth." Everyone understands, everyone agrees. Then work begins.

Corporate

By Nicholas Adams
Professor in the History of Architecture
at Vassar College, USA

An interview with T.J. Gottesdiener (Skidmore, Owings & Merrill LLP)

Corporate Architecture: term used to refer to the architecture for large-scale businesses or industrial companies, generally derogative; may also refer to the architectural firms that build for big business. The objection to corporate architecture is its anonymity; its scale; its apparent dissociation from or indifference to common social activity. Despite these objections, often heartfelt and sometimes logical, corporations and developers continue to build this architecture—and critics continue to criticize it.

This is not, of course, an old or a venerable term. You won't find the term "corporate architecture" in Vitruvius or Alberti, not even in Durand or Semper. It originated in the second half of the twentieth century, still used within inverted commas as "corporate architecture" in 1955, as if the writer was selfconsciously confecting a new way of describing the architecture of the American corporation. Not even the Museum of Modern Art used the term in their exhibition devoted to the *Buildings for Business and Government* (New York: Museum of Modern Art, 1957). And it fails to appear in *Architectural Forum*'s collection of articles on office and industrial buildings, *Building for Business* (New York, 1957). Like the term "bank art," used to refer to the bland art collected by banks and business generally, it has a pejorative connotation within academic circles. But why repeat the usual tired condemnations? Why seek out countervailing examples that only have the effect of reinscribing conventional opinion? Instead I decided to talk to someone intimately involved with corporations and their architectural needs. My goal was to try to understand the experience of making architecture for the corporation from the point of view of the large-scale architectural firm.

T.J. Gottesdiener serves as the managing director of the New York office of Skidmore, Owings & Merrill LLP (SOM), one of the largest architectural firms in the United States. Gottesdiener has worked at SOM since 1980. Born in 1955, he studied at Trinity College, Hartford, and Cooper Union and worked for James Polshek Associates before moving to SOM. As a partner and managing director of the New York office and one of two partners there responsible for administration, fee negotiation, and client relations, he is very familiar with the world of "big" architecture. Teamed with a design partner, he has been involved with many major projects for SOM including work in the Philippines, South Korea, Japan, Brazil, the Middle East, Europe and the United States, and projects such as Ben Gurion International Airport, Israel; the Time Warner Center, 7 World Trade Center, John Jay College and Freedom Tower, all in New York; and the Tokyo Midtown Project. We met on 5 January 2007 at the New York offices of SOM on Wall Street—an appropriate location, one might think, for a firm specializing in architecture for the corporation. But Gottesdiener's office is spare, more a cubicle than a place from which to play "masters of the universe," and the conversation is staccato, swift, and unambiguous.

Q: How useful is the term corporate architecture?

TJG: No, it is not useful and it is quite confusing. Who are we talking about? Are we talking about the architect or are we talking about the client? Actually, I think the term has less relevance now than ever. This term became prevalent in the fifties, sixties and seventies, particularly in the United States, when the Medicis of the world were corporations; they were the clients who had big ambitions, big ideas, and had the financial wherewithal and the political clout to do big things. That has changed. In fact, today the most emboldened clients are individuals. They might be at the head of a corporation, but more often than not they are developers who are looking for a grand vision. Corporations today tend to want to play it safe.

Q: So one problem with the term is to break down the relation between corporations and developers? Should we use the term developer architecture?

TJG: It is not totally black and white. There are corporations that have done and continue to do bold work. Take the case of IAC/InterActive and their recent work with Frank Gehry on Manhattan's West Side. InterActive may not be a well-known corporation, but Barry Diller, who runs the company, is a business icon. This is a case where the individual is better known than the company he runs, so it makes sense that he would hire an architect like Gehry, whose work is also iconic. By contrast, when we think of SOM's great works, like Lever House, Connecticut General, or Weyerhauser, we can hardly remember the names of the responsible individuals at those corporations and we remember the firm name, but not necessarily the name of the

CEO. However, I think it is fair to say that this organizational difference does not result in a qualitative difference in the design.

Q: So the issue is whether we have an organization led by a strong individual or whether it is simply a matter of the organization developing special requirements in response to situations. Let's address the question of the pejorative reputation, however we use or misuse the term. There is a perception that corporations (and developers) are not prepared to pay for good architecture.

TJG: That isn't quite correct. It is not so much a question of money as it is a question of what they want to achieve. As the nature of corporate America has changed, so too has the nature of the architecture they commission. Public companies, with all their oversight, demand that their leadership play it safe. Buildings they commission have to look good, be on budget, be efficient, and (and this is a relatively new requirement) they often need a kind of flexibility that was rarely required before. For instance, if we build a big trading floor we sometimes are asked to think about what will happen to the real estate if the corporation fails. Can it be turned into an auditorium cafeteria or training center? Can it be transformed into a use for another type of business? These are some of the questions we get. In some ways, boldness, at least aesthetic boldness, is not a trait that is always valued in business.

And, while this probably sounds like a negative, I don't believe it is. Not every building has to be an icon. As architects, we pride ourselves on our ability to make something beautiful within the confines of a specific set of requirements. This is no different.

Q: Let me pick up another criticism: that even when corporations and developers say they want imaginative architecture they employ value engineering and cost it out the design amenities.

TJG: I don't think those are problems particular to corporate architecture. Corporations think about their bottom line just as anyone does. As architects, we have clients and along with that come schedules, responsibilities and budgets. And that's as true for someone who commissions a house as it is for someone building a 50-story office tower. The biggest dilemma and our biggest challenge is how to nudge the client toward architecture that is better than what they think they want. This is a very delicate dynamic and it is always our greatest challenge. But I think corporations come to a place like SOM because they need the certainty that we provide: security that we will get it right, and get it on time and on budget. At the same time they know that they can look to us to push them a little in order to make the best building we can within their requirements.

Q: So this question of architectural design can turn on issues at a microlevel?

TJG: Absolutely. I think the days of unquestioning trust in the architect are gone. And that applies across the board, but particularly when you are working at the scale that we are. And by that I mean that there was a time when a client used to say "here's my program," or "I need a new building, here's the site," and we would show them the design four or five times and then we would begin construction. Today, we see a client on a weekly basis, sometimes even on a daily basis. They want to be involved at every point in the process, to see every nuance. This is both good and bad.

Q: Is there a danger that we get shortsighted design? The architect has to have the vision from the beginning and present it from the first meeting.

TJG: Well, that's true. On the other hand, if they get to see you on a weekly basis, they get to know you and trust you and to believe in you. You build the client's trust so that when you come into the next meeting and say, "Look, I had an idea. Let's push this," they will trust you. Building trust is the most important part of the relationship.

Q: Is it important for the architectural firm to have a designer whose name might draw in clients?

TJG: Yes, architecture suffers a bit, like so much of contemporary culture, from the cult of the celebrity. Having a name, a personality, that people recognize is definitely important. But, ultimately, as Mies said, "God is in the details." To build, and to build well, requires a depth of knowledge and experience. It is quite profound. The idea of the celebrity is of course quite shallow; it is only a veneer. In architecture, what should really count, is, not only design talent, but also an understanding of spatial issues, of materials, of detailing and of urbanism.

Q: At SOM all three original partners are dead and none was a designer. Are you competing with firms that are quite unlike you? SOM is comparatively anonymous.

TJG: All partnerships suffer from that problem and as a result you see the promotion of individual names within the firm. But in reality it's like going to a restaurant. If Daniel Boulud owns twelve restaurants what are the chances that he will actually prepare the food that you eat? Still, it is the name that has drawn you in there, so that is the hook. For a firm like ours, the individual is important but we have always stressed the importance of the team. And a team could be the architect with his or her consultants, or it could be a group of thirty architects that are working on the job within the firm.

Q: Corporations can also be rather secretive about their activities. Does that present a problem for you when the market seems to want to have names?

TJG: If someone wants to promote their building, that's great. But we didn't become architects to become famous and we don't do these projects to become famous. We do these projects because we want to make great architecture, to make a difference in the built environment and to create a sense of place. Publicity is nice, and it is increasingly important in the world, but it isn't our goal.

Q: I was thinking about the fine building SOM did for Manulife in Boston.

TJG: And one of the things about that building is that it has a great environmental story to tell, too.

Q: That's a specific case, I suppose. Still, the public—even those of us with special interests in architecture—have the feeling that there is a lot of building going on that we know very little about. It isn't even clear, to me at least, what "building" means to some of these clients?

TJG: Yes, I suppose. But you would be surprised how many annual

reports of corporations have their headquarters on the cover. It is interesting. We did a building for Bear Stearns at 47th and Madison [New York City] and they were very low-key about it. But, it is on their annual report, and in all their ads; whenever they publish something about an offering or work they have done, there is a picture of the building. It is not an iconic building; it is not a foreground building. But it works perfectly on the street. It has a nice shape and it looks great in the skyline. But nobody says "That's the Bear Stearns building," but the company does take a pride in what they have done and it has become a symbol for them.

Q: Is there a danger that the architect comes to see things too much from the corporate point of view?

TJG: Not at all. I think that actually represents a misreading of the issue. Compromise is a fact of life for an architect, no matter who you are, whether the icon or the partner in a large firm. As architects, we struggle with all the constraints I mentioned before—site, schedule, budget, etc. It doesn't matter if you are building a museum, a house or an office. Clients pick a given architect for a reason—because they have a good relationship together, because the architect has experience in the building type, because the architect has a good reputation. Perhaps there are clients who hire architects that they can push around but that is not the dynamic that exists here. We never feel that we give in to our clients. In fact, we often feel that we are the ones doing the pushing—pushing towards better architecture, that is. But do we have to compromise? Always.

Q: How difficult is it to work with some of the personalities who seem to have egos as big as their buildings?

TJG: At SOM, we always work together—on every project there are at least two partners and it works well. The way we have things set up, there are two partners to respond to a client's needs and, even though it seems stratified between design and management, it is fair to say that I often get involved in design decisions and the design partner is always consulted on business issues. From my own personal point of view, it has been wonderful. Yes, there are egos but that is part of what drives everyone to greatness. This is a cliché I know, but they put their pants on one leg at a time.

One of the great things about SOM is that you get exposure to these kinds of people. We make a point within this so-called corporate culture for even our young team members to be in meetings to meet our clients. Many are truly amazing people: John Zuccotti [Brookfield Development Group], Stephen Ross [The Related Companies], Ed Linde [Boston Properties], Steve Roth [Vornado]. These are people who are just phenomenal!

Q: My sense is that we all should know more about them. Whether we like it or not, these are the people in the United States who are remaking our cities. And we are terribly ignorant about them, their taste, and their vision. In our final moments, TJ, I want to turn to SOM itself. The impression of outsiders is that SOM is something of a monolith, a complex corporation itself.

TJG: At one time we did model ourselves after corporations. Nat Owings and Louis Skidmore [the founders of the firm] went out to meetings and saw the way American businesses ran and tried to model SOM that way. And Gordon Bunshaft [the most prominent designer in the history of SOM] thought he would be the kind of gruff, top-down leader and he trained a couple of people to act that way but, in the end, they were not successes. That style has passed. I got here in 1980. I came as a young kid recently out of school. I got thrown into this place not knowing anything about how it worked. And quickly, I mean in less than a year, I was running projects almost on my own, traveling around the world. It was just a phenomenal thing that people trusted you. People nurtured you—gave you work and responsibility to test you, to see if you could rise to the challenge. I mean, obviously at some point someone thought I could rise to the occasion because here I am. But the firm has also changed. Basically it is run as a series of small studios because that is a model that we have found successful as we've grown. It is all about interaction, both within the team and with other teams. It might be twenty people, it might be more or less. Is there a sense of hierarchy? Yes, but is not meant to be a barrier. The seniors are there to mentor. "Mentor" and "team" are very important words for any healthy organization today, whether a partnership or a corporation.

Q: Of course, American corporate style as whole has changed.

TJG: And that goes to the second misconception about SOM. It is a partnership and not a corporation. Yes, we have a lot of clients, a lot of projects, and a lot of people who work for us. But it is also about working with a small group, with a smaller team. In the world today just because you have a lot people working for you doesn't mean that you can do work other architects can't do. The advent of all this technology, its dissemination into the work place, means that many other architects can do the same work. We are having to learn that.

Afterword: That the term "corporate architecture" is in need of an overhaul goes almost without saying: the corporate plain style and the corporate individualists require a totally different measuring system, and two different terms. Gottesdiener's comments also remind us that too much ink has been spilled on those clamorous situations where architectural firms and their clients have disagreed or where the results have been unsatisfactory. More useful (though perhaps less interesting) would be studies of the circumstances in which architects and corporate clients collaborate successfully. Such studies, though, tend to fall to students of business rather than architecture—a mistake, perhaps, since issues of aesthetic value are often poorly appreciated or slighted altogether. And his observations confirm what we can observe in the newspapers: that names matter. The publicity value of architecture and the architect can be converted into further work. Finally, he reminds us that being attentive to the client and to the development of the long-term professional environment of architecture is a complex undertaking. When Gottesdiener became a partner at SOM, David Childs, then head of SOM, congratulated him and added the following admonition: "From now on, your most important job is finding your successor." Nourishing tradition—another little recognized and generally misunderstood aspect of corporate architecture?

Seagram building by Mies van der Rohe, built 1957–58, in a photo by Philip Johnson taken from Skidmore, Owings and Merrill's Lever Building, which was erected six years earlier. The two buildings mark the border between corporate and domestic architecture along Park Avenue in New York. Copyright Scanpix/Corbis.

Desire

By Henrietta Palmer
Architect and professor of Architecture at the Royal
University College of Fine Arts, Sweden

The title of Tennessee Williams' play *A Streetcar Named Desire* has always fascinated me. Whence this breathtaking collage of words and things? *Desire* is both the word and the vehicle that carry us and Blanche DuBois in the plot to her sister Stella and Stella's husband Stanley Kowalsky. In Williams' drama the streetcar Desire becomes the rumbling stone that sets the story moving and then objectifies Stanley's brutal lust. Director Elia Kazan's Broadway production and subsequent 1950s film version depict Stella's and Stanley's humble home as a complex chain of disintegrated rooms in which flimsy drapes, Venetian blinds and sinuous wrought-iron grilles inadequately segregate the sexes from each other and the city of New Orleans throbbing outside. A home whose rooms are tinged with desire. This is the *mise-en-scène* of desire – not clearly seeing, just glimpsing and sensing. Elia Kazan was born Elia Kazanjoglous in Istanbul. Perhaps his spatial thinking was influenced by the Ottoman architecture of his childhood, in which the sexes are spatially separated by open-work trellises of stone and wood. Be that as it may, it is here rather than in the thoroughly illuminated structures of modernism that the rooms of desire are rooted.

The word *desire* contains two possible antitheses: desire for and urge to. Both perspectives are parts of the genesis of architecture, the desire for creativity and the urge to possess. Desire is an established keyword in the world of commerce and media. Consumption is the urge to possess and, by the same token, the urge to create an identity of one's own. Commercial architecture, however, often lacks the true qualities of desire, which after all is its opposite, i.e. the desirable as the half-hidden and unattainable. Such are the properties of luxury consumption, but architecture is not commercial if it is elusive – a discussion which Venturi and Scott Brown penetrated nearly forty years ago with their twin concepts of high art and low art. Here if anything the role of the media becomes essential. It is through architectural literature and the architecture press that architecture is constituted as a desirable object of consumption. *Villa Malaparte* could architecturally epitomise the medial mechanism of this desire. Hard to reach, inaccessible and known to most people only as a picture, and a picture logically exposed as the background to an undressed Brigitte Bardot in Godard's film *Le Mempris*.

Is desire, then, of relevance to architecture today, apart from its scenographic effect and commercial motive force? With the presentation in the international architecture press of Shigeru Ban's *Curtain

Wall House (Tokyo, 1995), an iconographic image was created which burned itself into the mind with a dual desire. Geographically elusive in the unaddressed Tokyo landscape, like a latter-day *Villa Malaparte*, and with a gigantic curtain fluttering in the wind, separating, with the utmost thinness, private life from the dense urban environment on the outside. The *Curtain Wall House* becomes a substantial and architectural version of Kowalsky's stage-set home, a building in which city and interior, private and public, achieve an almost shocking interaction. And in the process Ban contrives to elevate the private expression of the villa to monumental stature – a monumentality of desire – in the form of the façade-high summer curtain nonchalantly fluttering out above the street, as if the city did not have its own stipulations of law and order.

The *Curtain Wall House* can be seen as a consummate example of architecture as luxury consumption. But Shigeru Ban's activity consists, and consisted already early on, of two parts – exclusive residential production and an experimental, or let us say voluntarily based, production, which took as its starting point the now well-known emergency paper housing, produced on a shoestring, if that, and financed instead by the first-mentioned villas. In this embrace, this union of the exclusive and the absolutely necessary, desire flows freely and both are coloured by it. The involvement present in the simple paper structures is just as charismatic as the more obvious and classical desire of the white villas. What Ban has succeeded in showing is that architecture in its simplest form can be an object of desire. He has translated emergency housing and commitment to the coffee tables in what verges on a missionary act, resulting in an actual awakening of architectural awareness.

So what about the streetcar? Desire was not just something Williams made up, it was a supremely real part of the everyday scene in New Orleans until the mid-1950s, and it was named after the Desire district, a poor and geographically isolated part of the Ninth Ward. This low-lying area was originally an industrial district surrounded by a canal, but in the 1940s it was developed in one of New Orleans' *Housing Projects* for underprivileged citizens. Desire got its name from one of the first streets to be laid out in the area, which in turn was named after the first landowner's daughter, Désirée. In 2003 almost the whole of now problem-ridden Desire was demolished and a "development project" inaugurated. In 2005, soon after the renewal was completed, Desire was one of the districts worst hit by hurricane Katrina.

Climate changes today are creating disasters in places, and on a scale, previously unimaginable. Building is one of the main contributory causes of the steady build-up of carbon dioxide in the atmosphere. Questions which up till now have been reserved for scientists and specialists are relentlessly approaching everyone's table and every architect's drawing board. More and more often now we are faced with situations demanding a new commitment on the part of architects, commitment of a kind to which Ban has pointed the way. Considering the great attraction among architects to the visual image of Nature's engendering processes, why are we insufficiently attracted by the proposition of making architecture a part of the natural system? Is it too complicated to be possible for a normally skilled architect? Can we find a middle way between, let us say, Laurie Baker's geographically apposite smallness of scale and Norman Foster's sophisticated eco-tech? Can we make desire thunder into the ecological issues? One thing is abundantly clear: in order to advance any further on a planet which is beginning to see its limitations, we will have to dress up an increasingly obtrusive necessity in desire.

Francesco Clemente. Light, 1996. Watercolour on paper. Courtesy Galerie Bruno Bischofberger, Zurich.

Doers

By Jonas Edblad
Architect, Sweden

A list of the people who have worked on the smallest of the buildings I have designed runs to more than thirty. All of them – clients, colleagues, civil servants, other consultants, builders, foremen – have directly influenced the outcome. If the project grows just a little bit, the list will also include politicians, credit providers and perhaps reviewers. Beyond this narrow circle there is an outer circle of people – managers, manufacturers, designers, software developers, teachers, editors and other opinion-makers – the list can easily be extended.

The architect is traditionally referred to in the singular. Only the client shares this status. Others are automatically defined as groups, "offices" or teams. To anyone with the slightest experience of the profession, it is obvious that this reflects an expectation of architecture as an expression of personality, of temperament, rather than the actual practice of planning and design. Even so, this gap between vision and reality is a perpetual source of conflict.

Sweden has many big architecture practices, a disproportionate number by international standards. This large-scale structure stems from an unusually large-scale construction industry in which the consultants' capacity had to measure up to the contactors when the Swedish *folkhem* was under construction. Today, big construction programmes are history, though the giants live on. Their volume leaves little room to spare for small firms. Construction projects are plagued by a constant fear of others not being able to honour their commitments. Size becomes a factor of security, because big companies are assumed to be capable of deploying bigger resources. For the same reason, relatively few people opt for the more insecure existence of the lone entrepreneur, preferring to remain employees for the rest of their lives. A role which rarely existed for graduate architects prior to the breakthrough of mass society.

The architect is both individual and mass. An anachronism in present-day society, the focus on the individual becomes a means of coping with an increasingly composite world of working teams, consortia, joint ventures and sub-consultants. To navigate this system, in which the turbulence within projects can seldom even be mentioned publicly, the architect needs to be skilled in both talking and shutting up. This may sound obvious, but even so it is specific to our way of doing the job. Within the project, information and dialogue are keywords. All knowledge concerning the project must be available to everyone in the group. This demands a disregard of prestige and a common image of the project and its implementation. This target

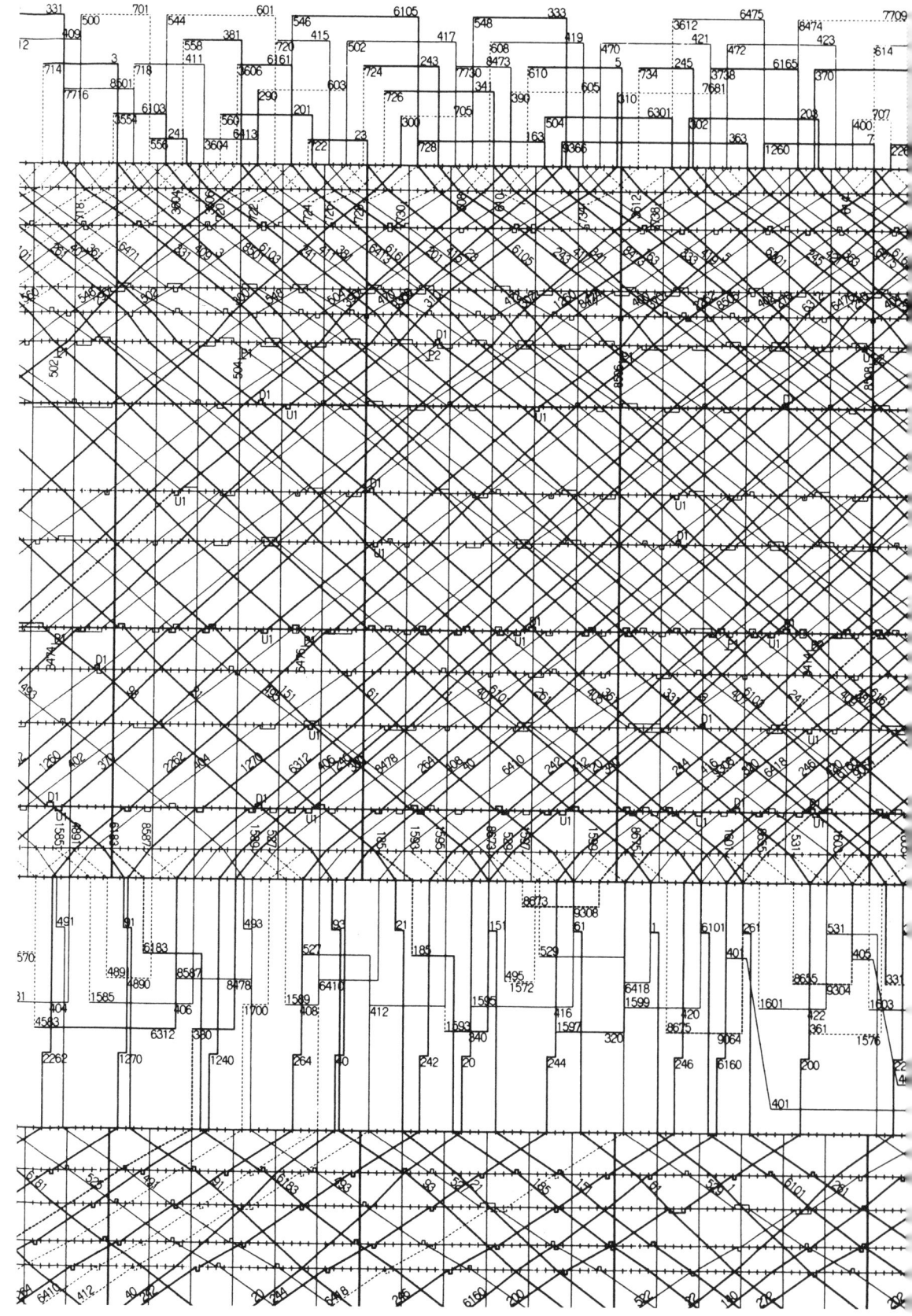

picture is the most important thing for the architect in charge to formulate, preserve and ensure throughout the project.

Disregard of prestige means acceptance of the fact that the best ideas are not necessarily one's own. Seeing the project advance confers a special form of gratification, which has nothing to do with glory. It is the cachet of conflicts resolved, problems sorted out and relations running smoothly. The office's projects and planning briefs begin with a core group of key persons, most often a handling architect and a handling engineer. These are the people around whom the implementing group, including the project's communicators, is subsequently built up. The group has to assume full responsibility for all planning and its follow-up. It may be expanded or hived off, but it is important that the core group should remain and be capable of communicating the project's thoughts and ideas throughout the construction process. In our experience, projects change all the time and changes therefore occur well into the construction phase. We draw the whole building, most often on a scale of 1:20, to grasp the overall picture and in order to weave other consultants' planning into the process.

At the same time the architect has a public role in which the finished or unfinished work has to be explained and defended. Here the architect instantly becomes an individual and is held personally accountable. It is in this exposed role that the glare of publicity is encountered. There is room here for a few individuals only, such that the image of what architects usually look like is created by exceptional figures. The doer, who heads the psychologically rather than technically complicated planning process, does not always go for that sort of limelight. The doer is happy in the group, listening and learning, carrying over experience from one project to another.

The notion of intransigence is among the most bizarre of the many fallacies in circulation concerning the conditions of architecture. If pride is allowed to stand in the way of learning, architecture will stagnate. Integrity is a matter of sincerity, not arrogance. Only with a generous dose of attentiveness and sincerity is it possible to transcend these notions. It goes without saying that this is an attitude which must be adopted by people besides the name on the poster. A really good architect always involves more people than you think.

Extract of operating diagram for 12.00 noon, July 25, 1985, Tokaido and Sanyo Shinkansen lines at the Japanese National Railroad control room, Tokyo. Printed by permission of Edward R. Tufte, author of Envisioning Information.

Europe

By Hans Ibelings
Editor-in-chief, A10, the Netherlands

There is no shortage of reasons why Europe, despite the continuing expansion of the European Union and other pan-European organisations, is (still) not united in a geographic, social, political or economic sense. And one might wonder whether this will change fundamentally in the foreseeable future. The differences between Iceland and Romania, or between Portugal and Finland, are – and for the moment are likely to remain – considerable. Furthermore, Europe is neither a constant entity nor a coherent phenomenon. The borders of the continent are changeable, and its history has unfolded and developed differently in each geographical area, each country, and within some countries even in each region. The background and composition of the population, social relations, political systems, economic structures, and divisions between rich and poor vary widely throughout Europe. In spite of this, there are identifiable areas in which a European unity, transcending the EU, is emerging amidst all this diversity and contrast. One of these areas is certainly architecture. Without dismissing all the local, regional and national differences in culture, conventions and traditions, and without ignoring the significant asymmetry in coverage between East and West, and to a somewhat lesser degree, between North and South (with the East and South as the underdogs), there is a remarkable consistency within European architecture. This consistency lies primarily in the fact that architecture is a quintessentially European pursuit. One need not indulge in Euro-chauvinism or a sense of cultural superiority to observe that Europe has set the tone for architecture for centuries. Virtually every general history of architecture is, explicitly or implicitly, a history of European architecture, and even when this is not the case, Europe is nevertheless the focus and often the prevailing standard and reference of any historical narrative. In most histories, after an initial review of the Middle East, it is Europe, and mainly Western Europe, that is the primary territory of architecture. The United States starts to matter in the nineteenth century, Japan and Latin America begin to play a role around the mid-twentieth century, and – apart from fashionable, momentary interest in places like Lagos, Shanghai or Dubai – Asia, Africa and Australia barely register, even today. Simply put, a world history of architecture, in many respects and for many periods, is at most a derivative of European architectural history.

The fact that, in European architecture, it is primarily Western Europe that has set the tone can be seen, on the one hand, as the logical result of the dominant role that countries like Italy, France and Germany have played in the development of architecture through the centuries. On the other hand, this dominance is reinforced to a significant extent by the predominant principle within architectural history – that of positive feedback, by which once anything has been declared significant, it remains significant for generations, and grows more significant through repetition of the process. The considerable prevalence of Western European architecture is reinforced by the fact that the historians with the greatest reading audience, and therefore the greatest authority and influence, were and are based in Western Europe – and the United States.

That said, Europe is the continent with the highest concentration of architects, and architecture. It is certainly not the only continent that counts when it comes to architecture: however, not only is there more architecture here than anywhere else (in the sense of buildings designed with care, attention and artistic intentions), but this architecture enjoys relatively high esteem. In Europe, architects are looked to, more or less as a matter of course, to shape the public domain, from public buildings to public space, from subsidised housing to urban design. Implicitly or explicitly, in numerous places in Europe, there is a prevailing view that the spatial and aesthetic qualities of architecture contribute, at least potentially, to the quality of life, and of society.

Partly because of this, it can be said, without expressing a qualification or judgement, that architecture is a predominantly European concern, as evidenced by the majority of architecture journals, which, though this may not be acknowledged in so many words, deal primarily with European architecture (albeit with the usual focus on Western Europe).

Most architecture periodicals do this more or less by common consent, by concentrating for the most part on the same buildings and designers (opinions on the importance and meaning of which are subject to the mechanism of positive feedback) – roughly speaking the kind of architecture that is a likely candidate for the next Mies van der Rohe Award for European Architecture. This unanimity is apparent not only from the selective attention devoted to a specific kind of architecture, but also from the consensus about what is the hippest place to be at any given time. In the late 1980s, the spotlight of architecture focused on Spain, and in particular on Barcelona in the run-up to the 1992 Olympic Games. In the early 1990s it was the turn of the Switzerland of the Swiss box, and in the waning years of the twentieth century the conceptual supermodern architecture of the Netherlands. There seems to have been less unified attention focused on a single country or region since then. This might be an intermediate moment, or a reflection of a possibly fundamental change – that the leading developments at the moment are no longer concentrated within one geographically limited area, but are instead emerging throughout the continent. Over the last few years, for instance, Irish architecture has made a big splash, architects in Estonia have been talked about, a new generation has come to the fore in Portugal, Austria has been enjoying a renaissance and young countries like Slovenia and Croatia have been making remarkable progress. The fact that at the moment no one specific country, region or city is the focus of architectural developments or media attention (which are usually joined at the hip) could be interpreted as a new condition in the age of globalisation, in which the classical spatial distinction between centre and periphery no longer matters very much. Thanks to new means of communication, that distinction has for the most part disappeared, and centre and periphery have become interchangeable: anything can be the centre, and everything is the periphery. (The latter, according to pessimists, applies to all of Europe, which they say is not equipped for global competition with emerging economies in countries like China, India and Brazil, and whose aging demographics will increasingly marginalise it in the global economy.) Interestingly enough, several of the leaders of the architectural culture of the moment are not to be found in the traditional cultural centres, the Western European capitals. It is significant that two of the most famous architecture firms of the moment are based in Rotterdam (OMA) and Basel (Herzog & de Meuron). Cities like Porto and Glasgow may well play a greater role in current architectural culture than Lisbon and Edinburgh; many of the leading architecture schools, and breeding grounds for future generations, are located in so-called peripheral cities, like Gothenburg, Graz or Gliwice. This is an additional indication that architects no longer concentrate (or need to do so) in or near capitals in order to achieve a significant position. Even when they live and work outside the traditional cultural centres, after all, today's architects are part of a subculture within the cosmopolite upper stratum of Europe, and it is precisely this that connects the most talked-about and most promising elements of this profession across national borders.

The free exchange of goods, services and people within the EU has certainly contributed to this, along with the Eurozone, the frictionless crossing of borders between the Schengen countries, and a series of other phenomena, from the Erasmus student exchange, Europan competitions for young architects and European tenders to the cheap flights of EasyJet and other budget airlines, the peripheral destinations of which have substantially altered the geography of Europe and elevated the status of previously insignificant places.

In an age of globalisation in which everyone can have access to the same information instantly, one's location has become much less relevant than the connections one can establish there, and in present-day Europe the conditions for connections in architecture are more favourable than they have ever been. Modern technology and all the options for mobility mean that no one has to live in a metropolis in order to maintain a cosmopolitan, metropolitan lifestyle. This has an impact not only on the cosmopolites who are part of European architectural culture but perhaps, ultimately, on the built environment as well. If a village can possess the qualities of the big city, and conversely the city can acquire a village allure – if, in other words, the contrast between city and countryside, between metropolis and village are steadily losing their relevance, a new European geography might emerge.

Everyday

By Denise Scott Brown
Principal in Venturi, Scott Brown and Associates, USA

Zulu kraals. Sand skyscrapers of Shibam. White, cubist Greek island houses. European Medieval towns. Row housing from eighteenth- and nineteenth-century London or Philadelphia. Early twentieth-century Manhattan apartment houses, seen from the back. Southwestern bungalows. South American barrios. Shanghai's lilong housing. Tokyo's mid-rise 1950s office buildings. Levittown. Strip commercial architecture at the edges of American cities. High-rise apartment districts of Pacific rim cities.

These are candidates for inclusion in the architecture of the everyday. Lovers of medieval towns or Georgian squares may not like to find commercial strips on the list but, hate them or love them, all these examples have in common that they are not institutions, palaces, or public buildings. They are not "special" – although some may gain an aura from their long history. Like the daily newspaper, they are the quotidian; people use them every day.

Some are, or were, poor people's architecture. Many were handmade artifacts of a folk culture and are called "vernacular" architecture, or "architecture without architects." These are easy to like, but others, such as shanty towns, trailer housing, "ticky tacky boxes" and commercial strips, are loved only by their owners and a scattering of a few artists and sociologists.

Everyday buildings are constrained by construction technology. For centuries their roofs limited their dimensions. In the medieval city, the rafters of special buildings could cover wide spans, but for everyday structures the optimum was about four meters. This module reads as a rhythmic beat across much vernacular architecture – think of the medieval town, but think of Levittown too, and 1950s Tokyo, rebuilt after World War II within ancient property lines.

Everyday construction uses methods that are conventional in their time and place. This makes for an orderly urban form, particularly when it is built by one culture group. The everyday is local, not cosmopolitan; it is not an out-of-town architecture imported by elites. And it is the opposite of the Modern architects' ideal of a universal construction system that follows the mandates of modern technology and therefore produces buildings that look the same throughout the world. Yet the everyday is found worldwide. And in major cities of Africa, the Middle East and Latin America, or in the mass high-rise building taking place in Asia today, a series of modern vernacular architectures does seem to have arisen, which uses local interpretations of modern international construction methods.

In parts of the world where one group – perhaps a colonial power – exerts domination over another, the local architecture may be ignored in favor of a more "polite" import. This is an extreme form of the tension that exists between highbrow and lowbrow tastes within a society; and it parallels the differentiation between formal and informal found within individual buildings. In most houses, passing from front to back entails moving from public to private and from special to everyday. You go from a decorated front door, through the room where the guests sit, and on to family areas at the rear. The same holds for civic and institutional buildings, where the public is welcomed in certain areas, but others "belong" to the staff, and are more modest and less controlled. And, city wide, the everyday forms a local urban tissue that is a backdrop to public and civic buildings, and is served by a public infrastructure dedicated to supply, defense and circulation.

Everyday architecture is not amenable to high design. Architects may attempt to imitate it, but their buildings will be recognizable imposters. The real thing is not controllable. Although its individual elements are designed by their owners and makers, the larger whole is not subject to decisions from the outside – except in general terms via zoning, for example, and barely then. But faced with this larger whole – a street in Venice, the Ginza, or an intense commercial strip – an architect may feel, "I could not have done better myself."

In many cultures there are transfers between the everyday and the special. Beethoven used folk tunes as themes for his symphonies and Le Corbusier directed "eyes that will not see" toward the grain elevators of the American plains. The everyday has its scholarly celebrants too, from Laugier's evocation of the primitive hut to J.B. Jackson's definition of a modern vernacular, or our analyses of the Las Vegas Strip.

When architects use the term "vernacular" it resonates for them with the cubist phase of early Modern architecture. The look of Greek islands or Middle Eastern villages reminds them of early paintings by Picasso and Braque and of Le Corbusier's buildings from the 1920s and 1930s; this association with abstraction makes architects believe that the vernacular eschews symbolism. But anthropologists report that vernacular buildings, even if they looks cubist, use group and communal symbolism in their arrangements of parts and their decoration.

We have no problem, however, in recognizing the use of symbolism in Las Vegas or on the Ginza, though we sometimes overlook the opposite fact – that this architecture is functionally rigorous too. Its signs are designed as if they were pieces of equipment, to attune to the eye in quite specific ways.

Artists, whether Post Impressionist or Pop, have turned to everyday architecture for inspiration in their work. Some, like the photographer Stephen Shore aim to achieve the "consciously casual," the deadpan, the art that hides art. He uses artistry, while appearing not to have done so, to underline the emotive qualities of the everyday landscape.

But architects must consider use as well as expression. Although we are unlikely to be asked to design a commercial strip or a Levittown house, we can learn from the everyday, trying to understand the relationships it maintains within itself and with its city and neighborhood, and asking whether these are appropriate to our new building.

The conventions of everyday building may be more suitable to our project than some of our inherited architectural philosophies concerning, for example, universality or "truth to structure and materials." When designing, we must also be aware of the interplay of values between our clients and ourselves. But, if we can avoid distorting the problem or outraging the client, we architects can legitimately hope to express ourselves artistically through our work. In this regard, the art that hides art may be as relevant for architects as for artists, and the everyday may contain clues to achieving it.

While designing, I try to learn about the context of our project and about the archetype – the generic form – of its building type. Illustrations in children's books and the landscape settings of model trains often show generic buildings and environments – schoolhouses, train stations, libraries, parks, main streets, and stores – and although those chosen are, in their nature, the most traditional versions of these, they can form a reference point for a designer. I ask myself how would our building type be depicted in those generic settings?

City planners exert broader, less specific levels of control than do architects, but if the limitations they place on the everyday are to be legitimate, they must understand the operating methods of public, private, and civic actors in the city. And they need to know the demands that all these actors who design and build in the city, whether they are architects or not, must meet, because they, not the planners, will create the environment. And a fine calculus of what should be constrained and what should be free is needed, if the hand of planning is not to lie too heavily on the everyday.

The urban designer, like an action painter, should form an inter-

active relationship with everyday architecture, and thereby put it into context, intervene by adding a public building or an element of infrastructure, monitor the reaction of the private sector, then respond once again. Faced with the everyday, urban designers, in particular, should abandon the concept of "total design" and, like the Pop artists, accept "the threadbare banality of the American scene, the jerry-rigged, down-at-the-heels seediness of our rural landscapes and the spatial looseness of our towns," and hope, through sensitivity and a light touch, to "recapture the over-familiar, making it poignant, coherent, and almost lovable."

John Brinckerhoff Jackson, Discovering the Vernacular Landscape, New Haven, Yale University Press, 1986; and Bernard Rudofsky, Architecture Without Architects, Albuquerque, University of New Mexico Press, 1987.
Stephen Shore, Uncommon Places, The Complete Works, New York, NY: Aperture Foundation Inc., 2004, p. 117.
Robert Venturi, ibid. (dust jacket)

Georg Stubbs. Lord Grosvenor's Stallion Arabian with a Groom, c. 1765. Printed by permission of Kimbell Art Museum, Fort Worth, Texas / Art Resource, NY, USA.

Experiment

By Marie-Ange Brayer
Curator and researcher, France

The development of so-called "radical" architecture was to transform architecture as a normative discipline in the Europe of the 1960s. More often than not working in the form of a collective, the "radical" architects (Coop Himmelb(l)au; Haus-Rucker-co in Austria; Archizoom, Superstudio in Italy and Archigram in England etc.) attacked the project dimension of architecture in order to instil it across the field of the visual arts. Since that time, architecture has sought to be perceived as a conceptual statement, a performance, an action. Superstudio uses the term "expanded architecture". The project frees itself from the rule and its codifications in order to confront society, to be a part of the present. The latter exponents of the architectural "avant-garde" from the 1960s thus claim that architecture is a form of experimentation, and they dismiss its constructive finality in order to open it up to a new cognitive arena. Architecture as experimentation is linked directly here to the notion of the environment, which divides up the architectural object as such for the benefit of experience. Jim Burns, who makes an inventory of these radical experiences in *Arthropods* (1971), evokes this "experience in the environment" in the same way. Form as such is thrown into crisis, and the tools of the project (model, drawing) assume the guise of a critique as the enactment of the codes of representation. The search for an alternative use for the architectural domain and architectural practice, associating architects, artists and designers (the reader is referred here to the exhibitions "Superarchitettura" in Pistoia in Italy in 1966, or even "New Domestic Landscape", which brought radical architects and designers together at the MOMA in New York in 1972) now proceeded against the background of the functional and rational dimension of architecture.

As early as the 1930s, Frederick Kiesler had already approached architecture as an interface between the forces interacting there, as a dynamic process rather than as a form, between man and his environment. El Lissitzky, for his part, championed what he termed "physico-dynamic architecture". In the 1950s, the Situationistes in France, including Guy Debord, argued that the atmospheric condition of architecture should be appreciated as a "situation", and not as an object. For Constant, who in his *New Babylon* (1958) develops the first planetary village, architecture is an artificial environment, in the midst of which both interior and exterior are permeable. According to him, architects henceforth create "ambiances", collectively and in an interactive manner.

The radical groups of the 1960s thus transformed the architectural project into urban experimentation, having recourse for example to inflatables in the streets of Vienna in the case of Haus-Rucker-co, or realizing performances and installations (UFO, Superstudio etc.). Thus, experimental architecture is something that presents itself as a new method of intervention in the arena of reality. At the same time, Claude Parent and Paul Virilio (Architecture Principe) utilized its "oblique function" to defend an "active" architecture, that is to say a generator of activities in its own right. "Architecture no longer has a 'model' of society to offer," declared Sottsass at the start of the 1970s, accentuating the notion of "public creativity" and sensory experience. The concept of anti-composition is also significant. In the review *Casabella* in 1970, which served as a vehicle for radical theories, Alessandro Mendini suggested that it was advisable to dismiss the "old concept of 'architectural composition'", which leads back to the individual for the benefit of "technical and creative action" in order to assume a "continuous experimentality".

The common aspect of these experimental initiatives is also their exploration of the language of architecture, the codification of which gives way to semantic ambiguity, as in the drawings of Franco Raggi. But they also relate to a new place allocated to the body in its physicality. Thus, the experiments with the inflatables are themselves manifestly an enactment of a nomadic architecture, the sole foundation of which is that of the body, constantly in movement. In the United States, Ann and Lawrence Halprin set up a workshop where architects and dancers experimented with physical space through the medium of the body ("Experiments in Environment Workshops", San Francisco, 1968). The group of architects known as Ant Farm, on the West Coast, approached architecture from the point of view of the media. They came up with imaginary situations, and they staged performances (*Media Burn*, 1974) denouncing reality as media "image". "Architecture is not something outside the head trying to push its way in; it is more like a layer of fantasy-reality somewhere between you and life" (Chip Lord, Ant Farm). In parallel, technology also assumes an experimental, social and political value: it is henceforth at the service of an architecture that is characterized by the ephemeral and the transitory. Coop Himmelb(l)au realized *Villa Rosa* (1967), a technological device as well as an assemblage of PVC bubbles, inside which visitors experience space in a psycho-sensorial manner. "Everything is architecture," announced Hans Hollein in 1963.

At the very centre of this approach, which is devoid of metaphysics and critical of any transcendentalism of form, is the notion of events. *Instant City* (1969) by Archigram is accordingly a city which does not exist as such, but which appears uniquely as a flux vector, or an information network. Certain urban propositions exist only at the time of their activation, as do the "imaginary architectures" of Friedrich St Florian during the 1960s, which are only visible when they are inhabited. It is difficult not to think of Archigram when Peter Eisenman declares that the rock concert is the only form of architectural event as a "new type of mediated environment which incorporates the audience itself". Likewise, Toyo Ito declared, "We should build fictional and ephemeral architecture as a permanent entity." And it is difficult not to think of *Blur* (2002, Switzerland) by Diller+Scofidio, as an architectural cloud, a veritable "atmospheric machine" blurring the contours of the bodies and of architecture. This dimension of an architectural interchange – physical, biological psychological – which already pervaded the writings of Reyner Banham (*The Architecture of the Well-Tempered Environment*, 1969), can be found today in architects such as Philippe Rahm in France, for whom architecture is an energy beam, a material composed of air, particles, etc., without any formal or functional predetermination. For his part, Didier Faustino divorces himself from formal or stylistic questions in order to envisage architecture as a method for the critical differentiation of reality, an instrument which, according to him, should enable us to "regain our consciousness of the physical world". Architecture aims to be an active interface between man and his environment.

From the end of the 1960s, Peter Eisenman also approached architecture as a conceptual exercise, questioning the representational tools, the drawing, the model, and softening their boundaries with those of constructed objects. His morphogenetic, structural approach challenges the identity of architecture and the notion of representation. During the 1980s, the "deconstruction" movement strives towards a programmatic deconstruction of architecture, as evidenced by the Parc de la Villette (1983) constructed in Paris by Bernard Tschumi. He brings into play a dissociation of architecture that is at once formal and semantic, which refers to its true process. Bernard Tschumi defends an "architecture of events" (*Manhattan Transcripts*, 1983), at the crossroads between several fields, including literature, cinema and philosophy. Likewise, when they came up with their eyes-closed design for *Open House* (1982), a projection of the subconscious,

Coop Himmelb(l)au freed architecture from the programme in favour of the dimension of the event.

Today, the research linked to numerical tools is concerned with the horizontality between the modes of conception and production. There is no longer a transcendent image, an image of representation, but rather genetic algorithms, the code, the parametric computation, which open up architecture to the arena of genetics and biotechnologies. These are once again notions of interactivity, of variability in form, which are put forward by these architects, by Bernard Cache (Objectile) at SERVO. Produced by CNC machines, the architectural object (model, prototype, construction element) emerges as the literal result of its conditions of manufacture, the exact visualisation of the computational mode. This horizontalisation of the procedures is possible thanks to the new machining processes and to the machines designed for rapid prototype production. Intensive, differential spaces are explored through a cognitive approach to architecture which is no longer an object, but a dynamic, elastic environment in constant development. Gilles Deleuze in *Le Pli* (1988) had already notably anticipated this epistemic transformation of architecture: "The new statute of the object no longer relates this to a spatial mould, that is to say to a form/material relationship, but rather to a temporal modulation which entails the continuous variation in the material as well as the continuous development of the form."

Space is thus cognitive and no longer represented as it was in the radical projects of the 1960s, which caused form to disappear in favour of its instantiation in present time through the dimension of the event. The current dynamic systems have dismissed the notion of the reference. Experimental architecture is no longer mimetic, but explores the process of its own construction, and draws inspiration for its development from the immanence of its process. Its state may thus be described as "gaseous", that is to say permeable with its environment. Experimental architecture at the start of the twenty-first century is perceived as a sort of membrane of elastic and intelligent space, a source of information, that is adaptable to domestic space and urban space alike, and reveals its "metamorphic" condition. Architecture likes to regard itself as an "ecosystem", a generator of metabolic exchange with its physical, social and political environment. The entire venture currently undertaken by experimental architecture resides here, in its performative capacity to transform reality.

Formalism

By Marc Treib
Professor Emeritus of Architecture at
the University of California, USA

It is form we perceive, not process or intention. If form is the shape of intention and process, however, form is not without significance. Form influences how we live, what we think, and what we do. Form is fundamental, especially if we consider space as an essential byproduct of form – perhaps more essential than form itself. We certainly dwell inside form, but more importantly, we dwell in space. Taken in isolation, formal values have only a limited return. But of course there are exceptions.

Without question, we appreciate beautiful form, but that appreciation is culturally and temporally circumscribed. To those who built cathedrals in the Middle Ages, the Gothic manner expressed religious fervor, a desire to serve God, and an aspiration to elevate the spirits of the people far above the level of their own rooftops. To Renaissance builders, however, steeped as they were in the classical antecedents of Greece and Rome, Gothic was a pejorative term – the Goths, after all, were uncultured pagans. Appropriate models, they believed, should derive from the more refined and polite sources of advanced civilizations. The perception of beauty is relative, and it changes with the times, the country, and the culture. And like aesthetic appreciation, the meaning of form also changes over time and with the civilization. To be vital, form needs to reflect social values beyond those of aesthetic practice. The American painter Ben Shahn once described form as "the shape of content." Ultimately, I believe it should be the content for which we design, rather than only its shape.

Formalism ranks shape over content. We live today in a time of extreme formalism, where form, and form alone, is the prime subject of marketing and designer attention. Any display of environmental or social responsibility seems to appear low on the lists of many of our better known architects – if those concerns appear on that list at all. In their place, innovation, novelty, and dramatic effect have become the desired ends. Fragmented buildings, sloping walls, drooping blobs – all exist primarily because they *can* exist, now given an easier birth through the midwife of the computer. It is a world of special effects, and like the action movie, viewer interest can only be maintained only by making the effects more spectacular with each retelling of essentially the same story. One must astound the visitor or user, impress with the freshness of the material or surface; we must marvel at the formal skill and complexity with which the building has been realized. Instead of addressing the contained, we worry too much about the container – a complete inversion of what Frank Lloyd Wright asserted was the true essence of architecture. One can treat space formalistically, of course: a crime of which architects have at times been guilty in the past. But despite these excesses, the concern for space better relates to everyday life than those of form.

Many of the buildings that receive the most media attention appear to have been conceived from the exterior, perhaps from an elevated vantage point, perhaps best perceived as an illuminated image in a computer display. Alas, we normally experience buildings from ground level rather than from the air, and the magnificent formal games obvious from above are all but lost on the ground. Comparing a view of a model of the Denver Art Museum (Daniel Libeskind, 2006) with views from at least two of its lesser sides – or those within most spaces in the building – reveals the disparity between the model witnessed from above and the reality perceived from normal eye level. There are other problems with object buildings such as these: they rarely contribute to a collective cityscape and often stand awkwardly adjacent to any other building, much less one of their own, irregular kind; they are difficult to furnish, and difficult to expand. Many interiors are merely the automatic results of the designer's search for an exterior, stuffed within the desired shape, often with only flat ceilings. One must concede, however, that a number of these formalist buildings are handsome, and some few spaces, like the lobby of the Lewis Management School in Cleveland, Ohio (Frank Gehry, 2002) are truly impressive. There are places for the unique structures such as these as there was a role for the medieval cathedral. The question is, which client – public or private – merits such attention?

Many, if not most, of the buildings we regard as "great" balance form with space, each set in relation to the human who occupies and uses the structure. The great spaces of a Hagia Sophia or a Chartres, or the more intimate spaces of Ronchamp or Fallingwater, equilibrate the impacts of container and contained. They also balance a complexity of form with the complexity of experience. In his design of the Kimball Museum in Fort Worth, Texas (1992) Louis Kahn neatly enfolded the rigor of classical ordering with a modernist spatial sensibility, creating a building that at first appears simple, but which is highly complex in its readings over time. The paragon of a "simple form/complex experience" building is the seventeenth-century Katsura Villa outside Kyoto. The frame of the building is completely orthogonal using a pre-cut and fitted timber structure infilled with panels of cardboard, rice paper, and *tatami* mat. The module is consistent horizontally and vertically, roughly three feet by six feet. The container, thus, is simple and unassuming, although incredibly sophisticated in its detailing and craft. Inside the pavilions is a world of dynamic space. Because most of the panels slide, and all spaces are fluid, and any vestige of a static architectural world has been banished. Equilibrium reigns, as does an overall sense of tranquility. Yet it is a living architecture, nonetheless. Shoji panels modulate congress with the garden, at times occluding certain vistas, on other occasions heightening their effect. It is a spatially dynamic world although the organizing frame itself is stolid and unchanging.

Rather than "form follows fetish," could we not look more carefully at an idea of content and its expression in form, space, and appropriateness to its environment and society? Rather than the ever more complex architecture, could we not return to an architectural sanity where a sense of a greater entity – whether that of the planet, the natural environment, the city, or the social group – enters actively into the consciousness of the designer? Form generates consequences; the consequences of formalism taken alone are even greater. Like those of the comic book superhero, these powers may be used either for good or for evil.

Giuseppe Sammartino. The Veiled Christ, 1753. Printed by kind permission of Cappella Sansevero, via Francesco De Sanctis 19 in Napels.

Future

By Hans Ulrich Obrist
Curator and writer, UK and Germany

Daniel Birnbaum, had this to say of the future: "If the future existed in a concrete sense that could be discerned by a 'better brain,' we wouldn't be so seduced by the past. But the future," he observes via Nabakov, "has no such reality. It is but a 'spectre of thought.'" I would therefore like to propose that any attempt to forecast the future is both a provocation to rethink the past, and an opportunity to better come to terms with the present. Similarly, although this article focuses on forward-leading trends in art making, exhibiting, distributing and writing, I will begin by discussing the work of a few artists who are recouping various aspects of the past; we will retreat one step before proceeding by several. Working through past gestures, of course, is hardly novel. In the 1960s, one observes Pop exemplars like Lichtenstein painting their way through abstract expressionism; before that, Cubists confronting primitivism; and on and on. For brevity's sake, perhaps it is best if we simply concur with Duchamp that art is ultimately a *game*, a continually articulated struggle between the present, the past and the future. According to this model, the only constant is *change* itself: this is a vision of history under perennial negotiation; historical truth as forever *in situ*.

What, then, of the future? To begin, we should emphasize that visions of the future pervade almost all phenomena: they (a) evolve over time; and (b), are many. The future, in other words, is both variant and plural. Generally speaking, we might say that the post-1960 art world has given way to an era of innumerable futures, relativism and constant negotiation. It would be hopelessly naïve to attempt an authoritative summation of this activity – indeed, I doubt any such overview is possible, or even desirable – so I will single out only a few of the most salient trends. Marshall McLuhan's famous media theorising of the late 1960s evokes one rather utopian vision of tomorrow: the "Global Village." In a similar, though less well known, fashion, Gene Youngblood's *Expanded Cinema* of 1970 articulated TV as an emancipatory forum for connectivity and viewer engagement. "It is now obvious that we are entering a completely new video environment and image-exchange life-style," Youngblood wrote. "The videosphere will alter the minds of men and the architecture of their dwellings." These sentiments gained considerable traction among Fluxus activities of the time and a first generation of video art such as that of Nam June Paik.

In *Futureways*, 2004, the artist Rita McBride solicited pieces of short fiction from over a dozen fellow artists, curators, writers etc., about the future of art. The contributions are telling. The majority mention biennials and triennials, though none discuss art fairs, a testament to the prolific growth of these events in the years since this publication; many dismiss the relevance of Western cultural epicentres in favour of those in China, Japan and, in certain science fiction variants, outer space – a vision consistent with today's numerous cultural expansions into Russia, Asia, the Middle East, Africa, South America and beyond; and a couple raise perhaps the most interesting issue of art's future as codified data. Laura Cottingham, in her essay set in 2199, said that, "Although today it is well known that the artistic contributions which are most likely to endure through time are those created without tangible form – words, dance and music – the twentieth century was the last century to believe absolutely in the permanence of art objects." She goes on to call it "The Century of Grasping" and dismisses its "false hope for permanence" and its retrograde fetishisation of objects over ideas.

Cottingham's vision dovetails with the legacy of 1960s era conceptual art and the prioritisation of information, intellectual property and systems-based analyses. It also squares with the open-source movement famously set in train during the 1990s by computer programmers such as Richard Stallman and Linus Torvald, inventor of Linux. This is a future of viral P2P interfaces and user-led progress, gaining increasingly widespread appeal today through vehicles like Wikipedia and YouTube. The art world, predicated on an economic system of exclusivity and artificially erected boundaries to entry, has been slow to adapt, but, as with the music and film industries, adaptation is likely to be only a matter of time. So here we have a future of data-sharing and an art institutional system that will need to reposition, even reinvent, itself so as to remain a relevant cultural actor.

Doris Lessing has recently spoken of a future without museums. It is not that she is fundamentally opposed to these institutions, but she is worried that their prioritisation of material objects from the past may not be enough to convey functional *meaning* to tomorrow's generations. Her 1999 novel, *Mara and Dann*, is premised on the aftermath of an ice age thousands of years into the future that has eradicated the entirety of life in the northern hemisphere. Her protagonists, long since confined to the other side of the globe, embark upon a journey into this now desolate terrain but they are at a loss with the cultural remnants of former Europe; they have no grounding in its decayed artefacts and buried cities. This is pure fiction, but she is nevertheless reticent that "our entire culture is extremely fragile" – that the more dependent it becomes on increasingly complex devices, the more susceptible it is to a sudden and terminal collapse. In fact, Lessing urges us to pause and reconsider the capacity of our language and cultural systems to proffer knowledge to those outside of our immediate public. This is a path towards the future led by pragmatic modes of communication, just as, in the 1970s, NASA deposited an archive, a time-capsule, into outer space, including newspaper clippings, images, objects etc., which became a potential vehicle through which extraterrestrial life may potentially understand humankind.

In relation both to Doris Lessing and to the context of this *New Yorker* get-together, I am very interested in how conferences can become catalysts of new forms of knowledge production. This concern also preoccupied the Polish author Stanislaw Lem in the early 1970s. In *The Futurological Congress*, 1971, Lem writes about future conventions, like our own, in which papers are presented, but read only in the most succinct manner as numeric streams rather than as spoken language: 13, 22, 831 thus become expedient stand-ins for real words or phrases. Lem's is a peripatetic vision of knowledge formation in which global constituencies converge and disperse, at once sharing information and developing new models of communication.

My vision is similar to Lem's in that I like to conceive of tomorrow's conferences as being less about documenting informed perspectives and more about *producing reality*. For example, at the Serpentine Gallery last year we held two Interview Marathons in the Pavilion designed by Rem Koolhaas and Cecil Balmond, with Arup. Koolhaas was keen to build an "architecture of content," and for the Pavilion to be conceived with attention to the conversations, discussions and events that take place within it. The Marathons were the natural extension of this vision: the first was a twenty-four hour event in which Rem and I interviewed seventy candidates to create a discursive portrait of present-day London; the second lasted twelve hours and was themed around the topic of art, power and money. The Marathons address the possibility of the impossibility of a synthetic image of the city, or of the contemporary art world, and attempt to map these issues in terms of both the visible and invisible. In this way they reference radical experimental models in visual art, architecture, literature and music and offer ways of connecting them; in Lessing's case, hopefully they also supplement the physical output of today's cultural producers with information relevant to those not otherwise familiar

with their work. At the very least, as Eric Hobsbawm says, they are a protest against forgetting.

I am also deeply interested in exploring a future of cultural innovation outside of the Western European/North American axis. "Cities on the Move," an exhibition I curated with Hou Hanru, was my earliest extensive involvement with this, focusing on the dynamics of the Asian megalopolis. The show opened in Vienna in 1997 and over the course of the next two years ping-ponged to half a dozen sites around Europe before culminating in Thailand. Importantly, the exhibition changed dramatically from one context to the next, and became an engine of site-specific architectural collaborations amongst key protagonists in both Asia and the West – Ole Scheeren and Shigeru Ban, for instance. 2006 marked the inauguration of a different project on the East: "China Power Station." Located in the historic Battersea Power Station on London's Southbank, the show brought together nearly two dozen of the most innovative young video and filmmakers now working in China: Yang Fudong, Cao Fei, Xu Zhen and Yung Ho Chang, among others. The moving image works were projected in the power station's dark, damp interior and will soon travel to Oslo where a second version of the exhibition is to take place this September. The show then migrates to Beijing next year.

In Germany, the author Ingo Niermann has recently proposed ten scenarios for the future of the country. Germany is also the host of *Whenever It Starts It Is The Right Time – strategies for a discontinuous future*, an exhibition held this spring at the Frankfurt Kunstverein, which examines the late Greek philosopher Cornelius Castoriadis' notion of "enacted imagination," versus the antiquated concept of utopia. The show calls itself a "collective," rather than group, exhibition and requires its twenty-odd artists to engage with the avant-garde tradition in order to propose new spheres of thinking, feeling, reflecting and exchanging for artists *and* art institutions; this is a future of agency and potentially novel working methods.

I have become increasingly taken with visions of the future in my own work as well. Over the past year, I have surveyed artists, architects, designers, historians, philosophers about their own opinions of tomorrow: the results were published in a book by onestar press earlier this year and a condensed version appears in the notes circulated at this conference. In preparation for this talk I contacted Liam Gillick, an English artist who now resides here in Manhattan, for a more elaborate scenario of the future. Scenario planning, and the conflation of art making, writing and curating, have long been elemental to Gillick's practice, and in 2004 he translated, updated and designed the English reedition of *Fragments of Future Histories*, originally penned by the French sociologist, Gabriel Tarde, in 1896. Tarde's reflections on future progress through feedback loops of imitation and innovation are fascinating.

There is one final project I would like to highlight: the formula list. The undertaking has the working title of "Out of the Equation: Roads to Reality", and is inspired by Roger Penrose's ground-breaking publication, *Roads to Reality: A complete guide to the laws of the universe* (2004). This is both a calculated and chaotic look inside the minds of some of our great contemporary thinkers. Such a compilation can never make claims to predicting the future but in contradistinction to the dizzying levels of mediation that today cloud the creative process – what the media reports, what press releases state – it shines an unobstructed gaze into these figures' thinking process and indicates what at least some micro-futures constitute. I believe that it is essential to comprehend such visions if we aspire to a better understanding of tomorrow. And as Douglas Gordon says, it has only just begun.

Gaëtan Gatian de Clérambault. Studies in fabric, Morocco 1918–34.

Globalization

By Carsten Thau
Professor of Architectural Theory and History at the
Royal Danish Academy of Fine Arts, Denmark

Technology, economy and policy are often referred to as the three main pillars of modernity. And indeed protagonists of the Modern Movement in architecture during the 1920s and 1930s tried to bring these agents together in a general reform of Western societies. They wished, at least in principle, to ally themselves with the progressive social movements and state ruling parties of their time. Their metaphysical idea of wholeness and unity may have led them to an excessive homogeneous vision of society, aesthetically as well as socially – a totalitarian dimension embedded in the thrust of the Enlightenment – but they achieved a lot by understanding architecture and physical planning in a major context of society and its aims. Meanwhile the great pillars have come apart. In the course of globalization, technology and economy remain as virulent as ever, while policy has crumbled. National states in some parts of the world still maintain a transparent authority, parliamentarianism, freedom of the press and legal guarantees for the minority, but on a global scale political institutions are lagging far behind, seemingly incapable of dealing with the great challenges of the day. At the same time the public sphere has been undermined by vast slum areas and gated or guarded communities, polarized urban neighbourhoods structured by fear. This decline of the public sphere, due to flaws of infrastructure or "Berlusconianism" (in which capital controls mass media) is taking place in a period when, for the first time in history, not only societies but the very natural underpinnings of society can be destroyed (by warfare, economic crises and social unrest). Because policy on a global scale is lagging far behind other factors which determine our lives and appears to be impotent or reduced to rhetoric, many observers have come to the conclusion that the ominous blind spot of the human race is the total effect of human activity. Policy is not only deteriorating with regard to the absence of strong international institutions based on the idea of an international civilisation, but also due to religious fanaticism infecting civil society or taking over the political agenda. At the same time America, in what boils down to a kind of democratic imperialism, is trying by military means to proselytise the Muslim masses of the world, creating hatred and terrorism.

The early belief among reformist architects in history as a great river running towards progress and enlightenment, must now be replaced by the image of the delta, where many local streams move in all sorts of directions, many of them backwards. To the heroic reformist architects and planners of the great nations between the wars, as well as influential architects in the Scandinavian countries at the beginning of the modern welfare state (the latest successful *projet de société*) this would have been difficult to accept, whereas contemporary architects in developed countries since the 1980s tend to think of their profession as just another "job" or even feel relief about the obsolescense of social engagement from the heroic days. For better or for worse they interpret the present situation as intriguingly complex, open-ended, opaque, fascinating and prosperous. The sense of being is light, and expedience is the call of the day. This expedience may be part of what Karl Marx described as "the great civilizing influence of capital", and indeed some sectors of society are extremely well organized, such as the economy of growth and the production of knowledge, cooperation and the production of social relations in the corporate sector. At the same time other sectors of societies are left in a mess. As for the volatility and inequality of global development, we have only in part realized that what happens on the other side of the planet today, will affect our lives tomorrow. The large emerging economies of India and China, which represent 40 percent of the world's population, may become destructive for everybody by manufacturing cheap products for the world market while destroying their own ecosystems. Nevertheless it is unlikely that we can ask countries like India and China to reign in their use of raw materials and resources unless we do it ourselves.

Globalization goes beyond what we normally understand by internationalization in terms of mass travel, mass communication by networks and a common destiny. There is no way back, because the driving forces of the economy are intimately connected with this process and because we all like the idea. The great challenges of globalization as we have come to know it appears to be environmental decay, monetary disorder, globally operating terrorist groups, global warming, global epidemics, social unrest due to extreme weather conditions, globalized crime, devastation of biological diversity on a massive scale, migration, military build-up in competition for the access to natural resources, and corruption. Neither America nor Europe can *unilaterally* provide the answers and provide the means for solutions, much less secure shelter for themselves and their populations.

Today, as all sorts of knowledge are becoming commodities, even the production of social relations and social cooperation, architects have enormous experience in this field and should be engaged in this, but with a critical angle which opposes (paradoxically) the social engineering of neo-liberalism. First and foremost, architects should be engaged in finding solutions to at least some of the above-mentioned hazards. They can do this without being stigmatized as idealists, so often the perception of architects in the past, because within a few decades citizens in all continents will demand from their politicians that they confront these issues at a global level. In the field of urban planning, architects can act against the decay of the public sphere. Developing alternatives to the polarization between poor people and wealthier people in the megacities of the developing world. And in terms of energy policy, find alternatives to the vast horizontal suburban areas of the West, which for their part within a few decades will not be sustainable in terms of transportation as we know it.

2007 became the year in which oil production peaked, according to many experts. In order to enter a very gradual slowdown. In any case production is unlikely to meet the dramatically growing demand. 2007 also became the first year in which a majority of the global population lives in cities. Finally, it seems to be the year in which hundreds of millions of people in all continents were hurt by or became aware of the extreme weather conditions. Not so many years ago a debate took place on CNN in which Mikhail Gorbachev in Moscow and George Bush senior in the US took part, in real time, but many time-zones apart from one another and both several time-zones away from the studio, while listeners from all parts of the world, north and south, could instantaneously e-mail questions to the studio. A German journalist reacted to this event by exclaiming "the world has become transparent". At least in some respects it meant the end of distance, as this indicated that the planet was shrinking. One of the first architectural representations of the world and the world market was Crystal Palace from the 1850s, followed by world exhibitions in major capitals. Today's representation of the world as a macro-interior is the world wide web. At the same time we have come to realize the truth in Buckminster Fuller's dictum about the earth as a green (miraculously) self-supplying spaceship flying among a multitude of barren planets. A carrier we ought to take care of. One of the difficulties of globalization, apart from a diffuse and pacifying sense of guilt among individuals, is its Janus head. We appreciate the mobility and implementation of the idea of a global society, no-one wants isolated populations. On the other hand, in a vast number of cases, this is taking place against an image of the yacht club and niche marketing, metaphorically speaking. Mass tourism by budget carriers, a means to democratize travel and indeed a way in which people become acquainted with other cultures around the globe, raises problems. Travel broadens our mind, it is part of the civilizing process of humankind. It is also the fastest growing source of carbon dioxide. Climate experts dealing with this issue on BBC World Service refer to tourism as not only the fastest growing economic sector, but also a major destroyer of the planet. Already two billion trips are being taken per annum and in the coming years this will grow by another 500 million. Tens of thousands of hotels around the world are being built at this very moment. New markets like China are appearing and exploiting their massive potential. China will become the major tourism-generating source in the next decade. Just as Asians themselves, who have never travelled before, will be travelling to experience the outside world. Tourism will exacerbate the effect of climate change. Global warming means that places that used to be attractive/hot will not be so hot in terms of business, as one travel agent sarcastically put it. How do we travellers get things back on track? In the first place by developing connections by train to all nearby destinations. The building industry is another very crucial sector, when it comes to the use and abuse of resources. Architects, planners and engineers, however small their influence, will have to face up to the complexity of all such challenges and present the public with new ideas. The traditional humanist architect, who is sensitive to everyday life, will have to integrate a wider range of variables without becoming a technocrat.

The most visible role of architects in the present international civilisation of economic competition is that of star architects branding major cities around the world with ingenious designs or creating spectacular high-rise buildings. Some of these architects are products of the 1980s when architectural theory emphasized the architect's role as highest authority on aesthetic issues (in a process of general aestheticisation of many parts of society) or as the creator of autonomous works of art. This perception, together with the remarkable workings of creative engineers, has increased the vitality and versatility of the architectural vocabulary. The conjecture of the 1960s and 70s of the architect as a humanist, among other things being environmentally aware, lost its momentum. In part rightly so, because there was an element of asceticism and moral policing in that period, at least in the Scandinavian countries.

Because the triumphant ideology of the twentieth century was neither socialism, conservatism nor liberalism in the traditional sense, but the collective longing for a consumer society at almost any cost among the wider populations of the world, architecture likewise has to remain "attractive", but not necessarily glamorous. The most obvious strategy under the present conditions will be to bring together the aesthetic, artistic drives of contemporary architecture with an elaboration and sophistication of the platforms of humanistic design. The expedience of communication and the material and intellectual capacity of technology, science and computer power that are at hand should provide us with tools with which to reorganize things without losing an awareness of cultural diversity or the wonders of architecture as an autonomous discipline.

Humanism

By Catharina Gabrielsson
Architect and critic, Sweden

The notion of humanism harbours an innocence that defies its problematic, even ferociously dangerous, content. This is particularly apparent in architecture. An architecture of humanism, as most of us agree, is a good, benevolent and well-meaning architecture; one that strives for honest, just and reasonable solutions for all of society. An architecture of humanism does not only serve the particular needs of the private commissioner, but also expands the programme to encompass the rights and desires of an anonymous public, even the whole of mankind. Expansion is spatial, but also temporal, since the notion of humanism forms a link to the past in continuity with its forms and ideals. Safeguarding ultimately human values, expansion even reaches into the future – as expressed in the vague and closely related idea of "sustainability".

The humanism in architecture is what makes architecture larger than the object. It relates the site-specific ordering of architecture into timeless and universal categories. Humanism is what makes architecture different from other practical disciplines; it sets it apart from technology or exclusively commercial enterprises such as the production of designed artefacts. It makes architecture into an end in itself, as a form of knowledge and practice that is guided by non-instrumental and immeasurable values, in short: as one of the "the humanities", an *art*.

So why is this a problem? Is it not precisely the humanism in architecture which must be defended at all costs, which serves as its consciousness, even its unconsciousness, in a reality dominated by short-term speculations and private greed? The notion of humanism positions architecture on common ground with, say, philosophy, history or geography – disciplines that are similarly concerned with notions of humanity, time and space. But on another level, it separates architecture from these other fields of knowledge, precisely because architectural culture (in its predominantly pragmatic fashion) so often fails to take into account the questioning, even critique, of these concepts that indeed goes on elsewhere. If philosophy can be said to begin with a fundamental questioning of the nature of humanity, architecture tends to take most philosophical ideas for granted, using them as building blocks in order to construct its own disciplinary house. Claims for a humanistic architecture are generally a symptom of reactionary thinking, where notions of essentially human values are used to legitimize practice. They are like flexible and multi-purpose putty, used to patch up the holes in the shaky foundation of architecture.

The term humanism seems to refer to something inherent in human nature, a certain way of living in and understanding nature and society. In traditional historical writings, the formation of humanism during the Renaissance marks the emergence of the modern subject, one whose nature is essentially good and guided by reason. Humanism signifies a new recognition of the individual, liberated from the constraints of myth, religion and tradition – hence it is interwoven with, and a prerequisite for, the process of individualization and rationalization. What separates humanism from these other historical themes, however, resides in its *moral* content. Humanism always presupposes the "inhuman", that which somehow deters from what a person would say, think and do as an essentially *good* creature. Humanism creates a dividing line between the moral and the immoral, and in its all-encompassing signification – defining what it is to be human – it exteriorizes the concept of evil. Thus ignoring the fact that human beings are capable of doing all sorts of things and thinking all sorts of ideas, even those that we might find destructive to ourselves and to society. Far from capturing a fundamental human truth, the normative idealism of the concept is a denial of the uncomfortable fact that we are capable of doing *anything*.

Taken to mean everything that is good about architecture, "humanism" therefore implies that the division of space, the representation of power and the designation of various functions are all techniques that can be derived from the same solid platform. It means that the ethical element is fixed and already there, prior to architecture, as an unchanging basis of common values. It implies, for a start, that there is such a thing as "a human", taken as an essential category – that is, regardless of sex, class, race, individual preferences, education and other social conditions. This belief can, as I said, at best be considered as innocent. But it is the very innocence that prevents architecture from recognizing its own potentials and responsibilities as a productive force in society. It separates architecture from those other "humanities" that are more concerned with the conditions of the present, the particularities of time and space, than of preserving eternal values. Paradoxically, it is precisely the innocent belief in humanism that separates architecture from art, where "art" refers to a discipline that has consistently questioned the legitimacy, identity, morals and means of its own discipline.

A closer reading of the historical concept of humanism, however, reveals such an ambivalence at its core. The humanism of Giovanni

Pico della Mirandola (in his *Oratio de hominis dignitate* from 1488) is not based on the idea of an essentially good human nature, but on the responsibility and anguish that comes with freedom (such as in the notion of the free will). Still arguing within a theological framework, Pico della Mirandola claims that man's position at the centre of God's created universe means that he is set apart from the hierarchy of nature. We are thus compelled to reflect upon the uncertainty of our existence, to use our judgement in order to *choose* who we want to be. But as with every received idea, the existential depths within the core of the concept tend to disappear. The troubling insight is met with a force, similarly "human", that actively denies all complexity. This force can best be captured in the writings of Michel Foucault, who in *The Order of Things (Les mots et les choses*, 1966) lays bear the system of knowledge in Western thought, based on what he calls "the phenomenological approach". That is to say, one that "gives absolute priority to the observing subject, which attributes a constituent role to an act, which places its own point of view at the origin of all historicity – which, in short, leads to transcendental consciousness". What he aims to do is to reconfigure the understanding of science into a theory of *discursive* practice. In Foucault's opinion, there is no such thing as an essential human subject that is the foundation for knowledge of a likewise essential, objective reality. Our existence has no such *ground*. What remains is contest and disagreement, settlements and convictions – a process in which the disciplines are formed through a division of fields of studies and operations. The notion of humanism can therefore be seen as saturated with the self-same Western belief. It is phenomenological in the sense that the sensory experiences and thought patterns of the human mind are taken as a universal and solid foundation for knowledge, and it is transcendental in that is depends on an *exterior* source (such as God, Reason or Nature) as the guarantor of this being true. Furthermore: it declares this epistemology as fundamentally *good*, with or without God's presence. And used as a vague reference to universal and timeless human qualities, it smothers the fundamental truth of morality: the fact that it is always part of discourse.

   A different understanding of humanism, and a more relevant one, would be to recognize our own doings in creating ourselves and our world. Our relations, thoughts and actions are the only basis possible for reaching an understanding of what a human being is. In terms of architecture, this would mean entering into a moral field of inquiry where the concepts, traditions and potentials of architecture are critically questioned. Less concerned with the qualities of man than with the formation of people's conditions, this is where a true humanism of architecture would reside – a vital component in the ongoing search for architecture's identity and legitimacy.

Michel Foucault, The Order of Things (London and New York, Routledge, 2002) p. xv.

Adolf Wissel. A Kalenberger farmer's family, 1939. Printed by permission of Deutsches Historisches Museum, Berlin.

Landscape

By Robert Schäfer
Editor-in-chief of *Topos*, Germany

As soon as an architect leaves the house, he or she is on uncertain ground. It makes no difference whether he is standing in the front garden and looking at the residential street or on a terrace, his gaze sweeping across a river landscape. Landscape – there it already is, uttered inadvertently, that confusing term, as scintillating in its variety as landscape itself. Why does it irritate the master builder so?

In everything from literature through art history to landscape architecture, landscape is the subject of both scholarly and pragmatic considerations. What is landscape really? This simple question will not permit a simple answer. Instead, any answer says more about the person replying than about the subject. The essence of landscape can only be discovered, created and formed through brainwork. It is difficult to communicate about landscape without first defining the concept.

Many academic disciplines were glad to try their hand at it. They have ploughed the field of landscape so deeply in philosophical, sociological, linguistic, geographical, etymological and semantic respects that rotating crops of landscape theory were needed before the harvest of knowledge could be brought in.

Landscape is an all-encompassing medium, surrounding us with serial before-and-after developments. The significance of landscape is not created by the maker but by the recipient. This simply means that landscape is what we see in it. And if the architect sees nothing when he steps out of the house, perhaps because nothing equals his creation in value, then the landscape may exist but lacks significance. The environmental historian Rolf Peter Sieferle (1997) explains the nature of landscape somewhat more nicely by doing so in a scholarly way: "In landscape we find the physiognomic oneness of natural conditions and their cultural formation such as they appear to the gaze of the viewer".

In its early medieval sense, landscape combined nature and the people living in it. It did not mean land as opposed to the sea but settled cultivated land. "Scape" corresponds to the German suffix *"schaft"*, which meant consistency or composition. Eventually it classed certain social groups together. Landscape signified a country in which certain social norms applied, without being regarded as the opposite of town or city. Rather, it encompassed the connection between settled land and social order.

Landscape later acquired a more political meaning, describing a provincial or territorial unit. The aesthetic significance that we are so familiar with today did not arise until the fifteenth century. A painted detail of the countryside in the background of a painting was called landscape, but the aesthetic gaze upon the countryside was not yet designated as landscape. This only happened with the paintings by Nicolas Poussin and Claude Lorrain in the seventeenth century, depicting an idyllic kind of nature that travellers then experienced in reality in Italy. Nature regarded from an aesthetic point of view still largely dominates the concept of landscape today.

If the individual's mental landscape is projected onto a selected view of the environment, landscape becomes unique and thus almost impossible to transmit. "I spy with my little eye" is a children's game that depends on recognizing and naming the elements of landscape correctly. No problem if all the players have the same cultural background. Naturally, we first have to learn how to apply the early medieval meaning of the concept of landscape to our developed areas, these being urban for over half of humanity today.

Landscape is everywhere. Landscape is dynamic. Landscape is no longer understood as the opposite image of industrially impacted everyday life. Urban landscape is cultural landscape just as rural landscape is. The urban wilderness has replaced the wild countryside. Industrial brownfield sites have become agreeable landscapes in their dereliction, accessible, unlike during the years of production, and accepted by urbanites as images of an up-to-date landscape in the midst of the sea of houses. Le Corbusier called them the "ordinary circumstances of the world". He wanted to save cities from their misery. This meant demolition. He wanted to see Arcadia in all directions.

Ideally, architects try to relate their buildings to the environment. Exemplary icons of architecture are Fallingwater by Frank Lloyd Wright, Mies van der Rohe's Barcelona Pavilion, and traditional Japanese buildings. It seems an inherent necessity to establish a relationship with the environment by creating gradual transitions or by swapping the interior and exterior.

Landscape is an ideal marketing tool for architecture. The view of a park or even of a lake or the sea increases the value of real estate, whether on Central Park in New York City or the harbour in Gothenburg. Stakeholders are only too glad to idealize landscape, even a mere excerpt of it. Because when everything is landscape, even the city and the place the building stands on, something special on which to project emotions is called for. This was formerly known as the sublime. Usually architecture is content with this effect of a beautiful view.

Borrowed landscape has long been a well-known and popular

device in garden and landscape design of both the East and West. Incorporating the surrounding landscape, mountains and trees in the design visually enlarges the grounds. Architects know this trick too of course. They are not doing anything very different from Dürer and his colleagues, who usually depicted imaginary landscapes in the backgrounds of their pictures. However, in order to enhance the impression of integration with nature and landscape, architectural photography moves landscape into the foreground. Often it uses only elements such as trees or rocks as natural accessories to decorate and frame the architecture. To such photographic tricks that constructed a reality, Finnish post-war architecture owed its enormous popularity. Finland's apparently untouched natural landscape formed the emotional stage on which the architecture put on its great performance. Subliminally, the staged trees suggested the menacing wilderness from which residents were protected by the well-designed housing.

In a way the house remains a cave after all, shelter against the environment and its dangers: wild animals, and cold, wet or hot weather. Landscape serves as something romantic to project emotions on, like a postcard idyll, and as a container for infrastructure and raw materials, beautiful and functional.

Edition Topos. About Landscape: Essays on Design, Style, Time and Space. Munich 2002.
Topos 58: Architecture and Landscape. Munich 2007.
Stefan Kaufmann. Soziologie der Landschaft. Wiesbaden 2005.
Brigitte Franzen and Stefanie Krebs. Landschaftstheorie. Cologne 2005.
Florentine Sack. Open House: Towards a New Architecture. Berlin 2006.

Marcus Larsson. Waterfall in Småland, Sweden, 1856. Painted in Paris. Printed by courtesy of Nationalmuseum, Stockholm.

Memory

By Juhani Pallasmaa
Architect and professor, Finland

Architecture is usually seen solely in futuristic terms; novel buildings are understood to trace an unforeseen reality, and architectural quality is associated with uniqueness and novelty. More importantly, however, human constructions preserve the past, and enable us to experience the continuum of culture and tradition. In fact, architecture is the most important externalization of human memory. It domesticates space for human occupation by turning anonymous, uniform and limitless space into distinct places of human significance, and equally importantly, buildings make endless time tolerable by giving duration its human measure. As Gaston Bachelard states, the "house is an instrument with which to confront the cosmos".

Architecture is also a significant memory device in three different ways: man-made structures materialize and preserve the course of time; they facilitate remembrance by suggesting and projecting memories; and they stimulate and inspire us to reminisce. Buildings maintain our perception of temporal duration and depth, and they suggest cultural and human narratives. Our understanding of the depth of time would be decisively weaker without the image of the pyramids in our minds, for instance. Buildings suggest stories of human fate, both real and imaginary. Even ruins stimulate us to think of lives that have already disappeared, and to imagine the fate of their deceased occupants. Recollections are situational and spatialized memories, they are memories attached to places and events. An experience of a place is always a curious exchange: as I settle in a space, the space settles in me. I can recall the hundreds of hotel rooms around the world which I have temporarily inhabited, because I have invested projections of my body and memory in these anonymous and insignificant spaces.

Buildings are also amplifiers of human emotions; they reinforce sensations of belonging or alienation, invitation or rejection, hope or despair. A work of art or architecture does not, however, contain feelings, such as melancholy or joy, sadness or ecstasy. Through their authority and aura, they evoke, strengthen and project back our emotions that we are attaching to them. In the Laurentian Library I confront my own sense of metaphysical melancholy awakened and projected back by Michelangelo's architecture. The optimism that I experience when approaching the Paimio Sanatorium is my own sense of optimism evoked by Alvar Aalto's architecture.

"There is a secret bond between slowness and memory, between speed and forgetting … the degree of slowness is directly proportional to the intensity of memory: the degree of speed is directly proportional to the intensity of forgetting," writes Milan Kundera. With the dizzying acceleration of the velocity of time and experiential reality we are seriously threatened today by cultural amnesia.

I believe in an architecture that slows down and focuses human experience instead of speeding up or diffusing it. The task of architecture is to safeguard our memories as well as the authenticity and independence of our experiences. Architecture makes us understand and remember who we are.

Modernity

By Hans Ibelings
Editor-in-chief, A10, the Netherlands

The word "modern" is easily used but difficult to define. Confusions of speech and misunderstandings, combined with the splitting of hairs, are inherent in the word "modern" and its derivatives: modernism, modernistic and modernity. It is therefore best not to say too much in order to avoid such confusion.

Modern architecture is a specific designation for an architectural trend from a particular period (between 1920 and 1970), which gave rise to buildings and designs in a certain style (rectangular, light and transparent). This trend can be labelled as modernism, except in Spain where this word has a different meaning from elsewhere; and what is referred to as modernism elsewhere is called rationalism in Italy. Practitioners of the modern style often emphasise that this style is not objective in itself but rather the outcome of a design method in which the function and construction together with the use of the latest building technology take precedence. Incidentally, architecture in which the style does take precedence could be referred to as modernistic.

Modern architecture can also be understood in more general terms, such as today's or contemporary architecture, or even more modern: as architecture that looks to the future and makes a break with the past. In this sense, "modern" is synonymous with new and contemporary, and is the antithesis of old, traditional, conventional and classical. Just to add to the confusion, "modern" can be seamlessly fused together with its opposite to form modern classical or classic modern. The former describes classical things that look modern or have been modernised, while the latter describes modern things that have become timeless, such as the famous Le Corbusier chaise longue. And to complicate matters still further, this piece of furniture can thus also be described as a modern classic.

Modernity can be interpreted as the state of being modern, but also as the mysterious essential character of society – modern society. Modern, modernism and modernity lend themselves to the addition of prefixes such as pre, proto, late, post, super, quasi, non and un, indicating the various stages of development and the subtle distinctions of these tricky concepts. For anyone thinking or hoping that we have now covered everything: a new cycle has now begun: a second modernity, a repetition of previous moves but slightly different.

No other word brings about as many stalemate situations as "modern". Bookcases have been filled with writings about the modernity of society, of the arts, and of architecture. Few of these books give a decisive answer to the question of what an accurate definition of the concept could be, partly because in many cases the inner contradictions are viewed as essential characteristics. No other conclusion can therefore be drawn than that "modern" is an ambiguous word with several meanings, and that these meanings are susceptible to change. They change because being modern is a relative concept and is connected with the opposite of modernity: tradition and all that is classical. What "modern" *is*, or is seen as being, is inextricably bound up with what it is.

That which is "modern" is now so well established and has been made so permanent that a modern tradition has arisen, which can naturally also be described in countless ways, ranging from the Crystal Palace dating from 1851 to Farnsworth House, built a century later, from Futurism to the Villa Savoye, from the Renaissance to the Interbellum, from Ledoux and Boullée to the present day.

The existence of this modern tradition means that being modern now not only relates to the non-modern, as used to be the case, but also to its own past: modern tradition. Consequently, every effort to create architecture for today or tomorrow is, more than ever before, relative to the past.

Nature

By Sverker Sörlin
Professor of Environmental History at the Royal Institute of Technology, Sweden

Nature is one of the most complex concepts that exist. Arthur O. Lovejoy wrote in an essay (1927) that the word had approximately sixty established meanings; this number has not diminished since. One very basic aspect of nature is that it is at the same time both physical reality and vital essence, the creative morphological principle that shapes form, which is very often understood as ideal. Nature, or to be natural, is therefore the quintessential norm. On the other hand, in Western tradition, nature has also been base, raw, and low in contrast to the immaterial divine, directed upwards like the longing soul. Architects, not unlike other humans, have been torn between the at times constraining norms of nature and the aspiring drift to construct beyond nature's confines. Some architecture has used verticality to demonstrate that distance from nature, eminently medieval cathedrals or some strands of modernism, where the high-rise tower symbolised independence from dull gravity. Still, vertical buildings inadvertently demonstrate the workings of the laws of nature, which illustrates complexities that immediately arise when nature is applied to architecture.

From the perspective of architecture, nature is at the same time marginal, even denounced, and fundamental. Already Vitruvius in *De architectura* (1st century BC) writes at length about nature: winds, climate, soils, how to find water, and about the architect as the necessary master of natural conditions. It could be argued that nature is present in all buildings and nature has been the eternal provider of forms and metaphorical inspiration of building in all cultures at all times, ranging from the grotto and the clay house to the curvilinear hi-tech forms of the turn of the millennium in 2000. What is built must be carried or carrying, just like trees and branches. Earth itself is a builder, and geomorphic features appear in the architecture of all ages. Even forms that seem intellectual, as in classicism, rely on natural principles. Geometry or Platonic archaic measures are as much part of nature as a leaf or a fruit. The column itself is nature just as much as the abacus decorating its capital. Order, essential in all architecture, is also derived from structures in nature. Vernacular architecture, from the Inuit igloo to the Maori longhouse, adhere to functional geometries as valid as those of the Pantheon or the Acropolis.

On the other hand, it has been said that nature has been suppressed in the very process of city building. Circular space – the camp, hut, yurt, igloo, tepee – represents the relation of each household to the entirety of nature, including animals, demons and gods. Orthogonal thinking departs from the parcelling of land and the consequential organisation of space as axial, squared and thus deviating from natural forms.

Architects' relation to nature is traditionally ambivalent. For a long time they generally praised it, harking back to Vitruvian origins, while during the last century they often adopted a distant attitude. Much of modern architecture involves transcending nature while operating within its confines and following its rules. We may distinguish between nature as a formative and as a decorative element of architecture. There has often been a presence of elements that are reminiscent of nature, such as curved lines, spiralling staircases, or the presence of animals and satyrs in Medieval churches. Greek or Roman gods and goddesses, frequently reproduced in buildings on facades or interiors, are symbols of different aspects of nature such as cereals (Ceres), bounty (Diana), ecstasy (Bacchus), not to speak of the decorative presence of the fruits, plants and animals themselves in buildings, gardens and squares (fountains, sculpture). But these features and creatures may have been a preoccupation that has greater relevance for the decorative arts and interior and garden designs than the architecture of buildings.

Natural ornaments have served as signs of the meaning or function of a building, such as animal figures that signify nineteenth-century animal houses in London Zoo, or lions that are sculptured custodians of banks. On the other hand zoos, greenhouses, museums, or other types of buildings or complexes where nature is on display, demonstrate the human control of nature, as do gardens. Much colonial architecture speaks the same language, demonstrating demarcation from threatening wilderness, whereas vernacular building styles favoured local materials and a strong connection between the outside and inside, where the latter meant shelter but not distinction, and certainly not distancing, from the forces of nature and spirits outside. Nature spanned the inside and the outside.

In modern architecture, nature appears in more pronounced forms. The trend towards ecological architecture and planning has precedents in the regional environmental planning of Lewis Mumford and ultimately Patrick Geddes. Characteristically it reflected, for example in Ian McHarg, the dualism of the city landscape that had developed since the eighteenth century. Kenneth Frampton went one step further and expressly advocated the role of place and the tactile in his "critical regionalism", which "necessarily involves a more directly dialectical relation with nature". However, in these and other attempts at architectural environmentalism from the 1960s up until around 1980, nature was still something to be found chiefly "outside" cities and buildings, whereas the ecological principles of green or self-sustaining houses were still on the drawing board. Early exceptions include Arcosanti, Italian Paolo Soleri's desert ecology experiment in Arizona.

Ecology is of course just one aspect of nature, but one that is central to the scientific understanding of new relationships between society and environment and to the increasing strain on resources, climate and biodiversity that arise with growing economies and populations. Architects have become aware, along with engineers and city planners, that ecological principles must be applied in line with the demands of sustainability, the concept established at the time of the UN adoption of the report of the commission for sustainable development, headed by Gro Harlem Brundtland, in 1987. With the overall aim of preserving nature, a range of sustainability principles has been adopted by architects, often demanded by new and strengthened norms of planning and architecture. A more vanguard example of this is Biosphere II, in Tucson, Arizona, a distant cousin of Soleri's experiment, but which belongs to a very different tradition, for it represents a fusion between ecology and cybernetics, and purports to create a closed resource universe whose scientific and behavioural aspects are perhaps more well defined than in the architecture itself.

Nature, whose status as a norm of beauty or as an ideal form waned, has since returned as a condition for the sustainability of all built environment. As such, nature plays a role in the twenty-first century that is as central as it ever was in the past. The challenges are enormous and the markets and demands seemingly boundless. When Bill McDonough, the famous nature design architect in the United States, plans the construction, from scratch, of cities and villages in China, he connects with his starkly nature inspired buildings in the US – the GAP headquarters in San Bruno, California (1997), the Ford Rouge Dearborn Truck Plant in Michigan (2004), with its half million square foot "habitat" roof, the largest in the world, or the IBM office in Amsterdam (2004) – and suggests that he will, figuratively speaking, put entire communities under a turf (or even a rice field) roof, which looks just the same as the landscape did prior to the construction of the city. Residential areas and workplaces will be mixed, energy will come from solar panels, and public transportation will be within easy walking distance. With the airport in the centre and a "Jade Necklace" of parks (Liuzhou), these visions mark a kaleidoscopic return to Howard's and others' concentric utopias of the early twentieth century.

This does not mean that there is any reason at all to appeal to a Romantic sensibility in response to the current state of affairs. Existing building projects around the world, including China, have so far paid little attention to the demands of nature or ecology. Huge development schemes in Shanghai, Beijing, or the infamous Shenzhen city – replete with signature buildings or entire city sections by Western and Japanese architects – are remarkably void of adaptation to sustainable principles. Another large building project in the early twenty-first century, the development of Dubai on the verge of one of the hottest desert areas in the world, boasts indoor ski slopes, giant shopping complexes, and a huge airport, serving as a new hub connecting the major world regions, all of which has been developed as if it almost negated nature, and which evokes old style utopia, with a shape and scope that dwarfs even the most hedonistic American indoor complexes of Las Vegas or the Mall of America in Minneapolis. It is an open question whether these urban designs, or the "cradle to cradle" nature design of McDonough (or something as yet unknown) will mark the nature architecture interface in the twenty-first century. Nature, while unavoidable as a norm, may be "shanghaied" into forms and contexts that would have seemed bewildering to Morris and the Arts and Crafts movement.

Nature has been powerful enough until today, and cannot be circumvented when the best examples of twentieth-century architecture were invented. The Forest Cemetery of Stockholm, Sweden, a UNESCO World Heritage site, primarily provides an experience of nature, where Gunnar Asplund's and Sigurd Lewerentz's low-key monumentalism only appear as gentle gestures across a speechless dignity that surpasses human expression. Although an architectural masterpiece in its own right, it also belongs to a rapidly growing class of phenomena, namely the green zones and patches of the urban fabric, which serve as conservation corridors or biodiversity-enhancing micro geographies. The architecture of cemeteries, golf courses, sports centers, city parks or even the backyards of suburbia, may typically belong to low or vernacular architecture, but they are manifestations of what has been called a "second nature" (Pollan, 1992) in which the human built environment is fused with "first nature", including the works of architecture, that must speak to it and interact with it.

Another concept which emphasizes the architectural aspects of this fusion is landscape urbanism, dating from the late 1990s. In a deliberate counterdistinction from the city/country dichotomy, James Corner (2006) and other landscape urbanists have argued that the blending of realities of the urban and the natural into an integrating form is also bringing together architects, landscape architects, urban designers and planners in "a shared form of practice, for which the term landscape holds central significance."

In the eco-globalizing era that we (seem to have to) live in, sooner rather than later, nature is likely to remain a strong presence, albeit dressed in concepts such as landscape, organism, context, or simply reality. The contemporary architect may not always have considered nature as an alternative; in fact, a lot of current tendencies and their trendy propagators have downplayed and denigrated nature, distancing themselves in line with conventional modernism from the perceived artistic constraints of green ideas. Nonetheless, nature is such an omnipresent and powerful condition that it defies any attempt to escape it. It may even return, at any moment and as strong as ever, as an aesthetic ideal. As the fundamental guide of form, function and order, it has never gone away and probably never will.

Anker, Peder, "Graphic Language: Herbert Bayer's Environmental Design", Environmental History 2007:2.
Corner, James, "Terra Fluxus", in The Landscape Urbanism Reader, ed. Charles Waldheim (New York: Princeton Architectural Press, 2006).
Kenneth Frampton, "Towards a Critical Regionalism: Six Points for an Architecture of Resistance", in The Anti-Aesthetic: Essays on Postmodern Culture, ed. Hal Foster (Seattle, WA: Bay Press, 1983).
Lovejoy, Arthur O., "Nature", Language Notes (1927).
McDonough, William, The Hannover Principles: Design for Sustainability (New York: William McDonough Architects, 1992).
McHarg, Ian, Design With Nature (New York: Natural History Press, 1969).
Pearman, Hugh & Andrew Whalley: The Architecture of Eden, with a foreword by Sir Nicholas Grimshaw (London 2003: Eden Project Books).
Pollan, Michael, Second Nature: A Gardener's Education (New York: Dell, 1992).
Portoghesi, Paolo, Nature and Architecture (London: Thames & Hudson, 2000).
Sörlin, Sverker, "Nature", Dictionary of the History of Science, ed. Arne Hessenbruch (London: Edward Arnold, 2000).

The Mauvoisin dam on the Dranse de Bagnes in Switzerland from 1958. Photo printed by permission of Pöyry Energy AG, Switzerland.

Nordic

By Nils-Ole Lund
Architect and author, Denmark

Viewed from outside, the Nordic countries are often perceived as a single entity. Even though they cover large geographical areas with great topographical variations, historically they are linked together both linguistically and culturally. The Nordic area (*Norden*) consists of Iceland, Norway, Finland, Sweden and Denmark, plus the autonomous regions constituted by Greenland, the Faeroes and the Åland Islands.

Despite a history of numerous internecine wars, over the past hundred years these countries have evolved a common model of government and society: the Nordic welfare state. As small and relatively homogeneous nations, they have been in a position to build up parliamentary democracies with state-financed welfare benefits and large public sectors, but still with open economies and strong cultural links with other countries.

The involvement of agrarian and labour movements created massive popular support for a political system characterised by the peaceful resolution of disputes.

Because of these relatively uniform conditions, architectural developments in the Nordic countries have also run parallel. Nordic architects have shifted more or less simultaneously from historicism to National Romanticism, from Romanticism to Neo-Classicism, from Neo-Classicism to Functionalism (the Nordic term for Modernism) and from doctrinaire Functionalism to "modern" Modernism. This makes Nordic buildings easy to date, because nearly all architects fell in with the demands of the age and their profession. And another thing the Nordic countries have in common is that their architecture can be described as a cultural import, with the original ideas – whether coming from the Bauhaus, the USA or the Italian Rationalists – being modified in the process.

When Functionalism achieved its pan-Nordic breakthrough in about 1930, architecture became an image of social and democratic development. As the Swedish art historian Gregor Paulsson put it, the new vocabulary became an emancipatory style and function an expression of the desire for equality. Typically, therefore, Nordic architecture can be described exclusively with reference to examples of public sector housing production.

Nordic architecture and utility production grew famous in the 1950s under the name of Scandinavian Design. The secret of success lay in a combination of good workmanship, user-friendly design and aesthetic elegance. Architects like Arne Jacobsen, Alvar Aalto, Jørn Utzon and Ralph Erskine became world-famous.

During the past decade, growing prosperity and changing political trends have reduced the social aspect of modern architecture. Neo-Modernism, now virtually paramount, has become a style instead of a summary movement of ideas.

However, contemporary architecture clearly requires nuances. The global climatic threat shows that a building must necessarily adjust to local conditions of terrain and climate, i.e. be in harmony with the conditions of the place or, in the words of Louis Kahn, be what a building wants to be.

There is no question here of a national architecture, a construction in which coherence is established between earth, language, history and architecture, but rather of an endeavour to create buildings which self-evidently grow out of the conditions of the place. In other words, a continuation of the Nordic tradition of pragmatic solutions to international problems.

An example of this pragmatism is the Nordic diplomatic quarter on Tiergarten in Berlin. Although they do not share the same foreign policy, the Nordic countries have set up a joint representation in the German capital. A curvilinear wall of bronze slats with an Aalto-like curvature surrounds the five embassy buildings, which surround a piazza that imitates the water between their separate countries. Individual architecture has thus been governed by the overarching plan, and the values and norms reflected by the architectural idiom are surprisingly uniform. But the practised eye will recognise local traits in the fashioning of details and the use of materials.

Esko Männikkö. Savukoski, 1994. Printed by courtesy of the artist.

Organic

By Peter Blundell Jones
Architect and critic, UK

Like many other broad categories in architecture, "organic" has carried various meanings which have changed over time. In everyday life it is now associated with foods and farming, giving it a health-conscious and slightly sanctimonious air, but also linking it with the sustainability of life on this planet. In architecture it now tends to be used somewhat superficially to label buildings with curved or irregular forms or ones which seem in some way to be natural. Only a century ago, however, "organic" was a rallying cry for an alternative tradition in architecture. It began with Louis Sullivan and Frank Lloyd Wright at the end of the nineteenth century when they set up their "organic architecture" as an alternative to the academic classical tradition. For Sullivan the biological notion of fitness for purpose and appropriateness of structure led to the claim that form should follow function, and ornament, which was still considered to be essential at that time, had to be refounded in nature instead of following historical precedent. Less concerned with ornament though without eschewing it altogether, Wright followed Sullivan's functionalism. He further stressed that a building should relate to site and landscape, a house being "not of a hill but on a hill." He spoke of "the nature of materials" and of "the thing growing out of the nature of the thing", implying parallels with natural growth.

In Europe, William Morris had described Gothic architecture approvingly as "organic", and art-nouveau architects of the next generation like Henri van de Velde also cited the Gothic, producing work which had supposedly been inspired by the flowing curves of nature and the sense of empathy which was thus transmitted. In the 1920s Erich Mendelsohn spoke of his buildings as "organisms" and Hugo Häring provided an elaborated theory of "organic building" in which the organic is opposed to the geometric approach, the latter being seen as imposed and artificial as opposed to the putatively natural character of the organic. He claimed that the free development of architecture had been curtailed by an obsession with geometry, evidently reacting against the rules of composition, which were based on the *beaux arts* at that time. For Häring it was not so much a question of choosing a vocabulary of shapes as of "discovering" truly appropriate forms for buildings. Each building should be implied by site and programme, he believed, and one should work from the inside out rather than from the outside in – on questions of organisation rather than facade. It was not merely functional efficiency that Häring sought – though he wanted that too – but an individual identity for each building which was fully appropriate to place and purpose. In this respect, he had much in common with his protégé Hans Scharoun and with Scandinavian contemporaries such as Gunnar Asplund and Alvar Aalto. The idea that the building has a kind of inner being or *Wesen* lies at the heart of this approach.

Besotted with Frank Lloyd Wright, the young Italian critic Bruno Zevi published his alternative history *Towards an Organic Architecture* in 1945 (English edition 1949) setting up organic as an alternative to the orthodoxy of the so-called international style. Nervi noted strong parallels between the work of Wright and that of Aalto and mentioned Asplund and Mendelsohn, but he omitted the then unknown work of Häring and Scharoun which would have strengthened his case. Since then the gaps have been filled and the case added to by other architects and historians, but the polemical power of the organic as an alternative tradition has been somewhat blunted by the collapse of its international style opponent and the subsequent confusion of postmodernism. Architects as distinguished as Günter Behnisch, Ralph Erskine and Enric Miralles have pursued what could be regarded as an "organic" direction without ever having to declare a common interest, and this could be considered a victory for the organic. Response to site, function, materials and other contingent conditions has led to architecture that would always be specific, appropriate and different, but this has also meant that the organic tradition has always tended towards diversity and differentiation as opposed to integration. The demand for specificity further implies a necessary appreciation within the given context, and by the same token denies universal relevance. It is therefore difficult for organic architecture ever to become normative in the way of the academic classical tradition or of the international style, as to do so it would have to defeat its own objects.

If a clear historical marker of the organic tendency is required, the contrast between specific and the universal appears at its most extreme between the work of Häring and that of Mies. The former always drew on the content of the brief as much as possible, while the latter ignored it – sometimes to a dangerous extent – in favour of an ideal and generalised flexibility. Thus it is no accident to find Häring in the mid 1920s revelling in the minutiae of feeding and caring for animals in his masterpiece, Garkau farm, while Mies reached the height of his early fame with a functionless and almost briefless monument like the Barcelona Pavilion. The same contrast reappeared later at the Kulturforum in post-war Berlin, where Mies built as the New National Gallery a revised version of his earlier HQ for Bacardi in Cuba – a change of site, function, climate, country, even material – while next door Scharoun had provided the most compelling twentieth-century model for the concert hall. In its powerful celebration of the concert ritual, of engagement in music, and of fine adjustment of acoustics, the Philharmonie is an outstanding piece of organic architecture. Its use for any other purpose would of course be unthinkable.

Louis Sullivan, Kindergarten Chats, Dover, New York, 1979.
Frank Lloyd Wright, Organic Architecture, preface to Wasmuth Portfolio 1910, also Organic Architecture, Architects' Journal August 1936.
See his 1923 lecture in Amsterdam, published in translation in Erich Mendelsohn, Erich Mendelsohn Complete works of the Architect, Triangle Architectural Publishing, 1992.
Häring's key essay is Wege zur Form, published in Die Form 1925, see translated extracts and Commentary in Peter Blundell Jones, Hugo Häring: The Organic versus the Geometric, Menges 1999, pp. 77–82.
Ibid, pp. 150–162.
See Peter Blundell Jones, Gunnar Asplund, Phaidon, London, 2006.
Bruno Zevi, Towards an Organic Architecture, Faber & Faber, London, 1949.
C.A. St John Wilson, The Other Tradition of Modern Architecture Academy Editions London 1995.
See Peter Blundell Jones, Günter Behnisch, Birkhäuser, Berlin 2000.
See Peter Blundell Jones and Eamonn Canniffe, Modern Architecture Through Case Studies 1945–1990, Architectural Press, Oxford, 2007, Chapter 11.
See Peter Blundell Jones, Enric Miralles C.N.A.R., Alicante, Menges 1995.
See Peter Blundell Jones, Modern Architecture Through Case Studies, Architectural Press, Oxford, 2002, Chapters 1 and 2.
Ibid Chapters 13 and 14. See also Peter Blundell Jones, Hans Scharoun, Phaidon, London, 1995, pp. 174–195.

Ornament

By Irénée Scalbert
Architecture critic, UK

In a celebrated passage in *Dead Souls*, Nikolai Gogol describes a strange castle set within an unkempt wasteland. Cracks in the walls of the castle expose the naked plastering and lath. All but two windows are shuttered over. Behind the building, appearing like a decrepit invalid, the garden stretches in the distance and loses itself in an open field. It has gone wild and in its wilderness lends a picturesque note to a place that would otherwise be desolate and stale. Everything, Gogol remarks, is as beautiful as neither Nature nor art alone could conceive. Nature lightens masses, it does away with the coarse regularity of naked plans, and it bestows warmth onto everything that had been "created amid the frigidity of a measured purity and tidiness."

The scene is an appropriate metaphor for the return of ornament in architecture. This is not to suggest that the source of all ornament is in nature, but more simply to compare the wilderness that overwhelmed the estate, its naked plan, its purity and its tidiness, with the recent growth of ornament from within the cracks of Modernism. Architects may still hanker after concepts, but these appear increasingly arbitrary. They may still paper over ideological voids with theories, but these seldom have purchase on ordinary reality. By contrast, the candour with which they increasingly acknowledge the demands of the senses seems to be of far greater consequence.

Few essays have been more present in the last decade than Adolf Loos's "Ornament and Crime". Modern society, Loos claimed, had become incapable of inventing ornament. Overworked by industry, overfed by affluence, ornament had lost its organic relationship to culture. The decoration on dishes that makes peacocks, pheasants and lobsters seem more appetizing had the opposite effect on Loos: "I eat roast beef." Le Corbusier, too, was nauseated by the decorative arts of his time. For all his professed love of Rabelais, he felt sick at the "evocation of Bernard Palissy", a potter who, in the sixteenth century, actually moulded the very fish and fowl that Loos refused to eat upon dishes which he then coated in emerald and turquoise enamel.

Ornament signified a lack of morality, manifest for instance in the tattoos of the Papuans – for how could a Papuan be moral? Conversely, its absence represented morality recovered. More than this, it was a sign of intellectual power – for how could a Papuan compose a work like Beethoven's ninth symphony? Never mind the parochial nature of the argument. More interesting is what logically follows from it: the presence of ornament must necessarily indicate a lack of intellectual power. But why should decorative forms, unlike other forms, be contrary to abstract thought was not explained.

The idea remains with us in the assumption that, while the naked plan, the plan as generator is conceived in the central realm of intelligence, ornament merely grows in the outer province of the senses. What happens, though, when the plan is not merely naked but, in a profound sense, absent? What happens when the plastering of concepts and the lath of theories become exposed? No injection of Gottfried Semper, the orthodoxy of the moment, could fill the cracks. High on text, one might attempt to cover, protect and enclose, as Semper more or less said of the idea of textile (and Herzog & de Meuron more or less do this in the new stadium for Beijing) with a ball of string. The entire corpus of architecture has become decorative. Its appearance is decorative, its plans are decorative; so are its techniques. Even its exegesis – the elaborate string of words with which it is often dressed – is decorative. No architecture better represents this immanence of ornament than that of Zaha Hadid: drawing, structure, form, surface all cohere in a single logic of sensation.

Even the work of SANAA can be deceiving. Perhaps the least decorated of all recent architecture, it is to white what Mies was to black – or it seems to be. But scratch the surface (the thinness of which should in itself give one pause for thought) and ornamental qualities shine forth. From without, openings contribute colourless, decorative compositions of gloss on matt. From within, objects from everyday life – Persian carpets, modern chairs, flowerpots, mats, quilts… – become parts in an elaborate decor behind which the body of the house recedes as it were out of substance. It is as if the art of inhabitation cultivated by the Smithsons and inspired by Japan had taken root in its country of origin and produced a variant of the art of *ikebana*. Life itself has become an ornament.

Thus Modernism ends with a flourish of ornament. So did Classicism in the eighteenth century. From the 1720s onwards, rococo architects like Ange-Jacques Gabriel also showed a marked preference for white, which they applied as the lightest of colours. They removed classical orders from facades, composition being limited, as in SANAA's work, to the arrangement of openings. Then, like today, sensibility presided over a state of mind that was mainly sceptical and critical.

The erosion of tectonic principles and of rules of composition gave *carte blanche* for the proliferation of ornament. Large areas of wall were left open for plastic and tactile experiments, the best-known among them being the *rocaille,* which has been described as "an ornament of no particular shape composed of a non-existent substance." Mannerist bandwork, arabesque and grotesque, foliage and shellwork fused together in a substance that surpassed all former ornaments in malleability.

Nothing better represents this triumph of ornament in the eighteenth century than the apogee of lace in the same period. Until then, lacemaking had been limited to the cuffs, collars and ruffs that flowed out and over darker items of clothing and created, around the head and the wrists, a transparency which managed "visual and almost musical transitions between the face, the fabric and space." Like the ornament that overwhelmed the classical orders, lace eventually covered whole garments and became a material for dresses. It was, too, an ornament for altars, tabernacles and the clothes of priests. In short it became the attribute of choice for everything that was most lovable, be it erotic or sacred.

In the recent past, three projects have referred to lace, two of them directly. Adjoining the old town centre of the city of Bruges, once famous for its lacemaking, the 1998 competition design for a concert hall by Neutelings Riedijk was to be clad with an "abstract openwork decorative pattern" – all terms that are applied to lace – clearly derived from a piece of fabric. In Nottingham, another centre of lacemaking, the centre for contemporary art (CCAN) designed by Caruso St John will be draped with "a coat of lace". In Leicester, once well-known for its textile industry, the curtain wall of the new John Lewis department store was designed by FOA to perform in the manner of "lace curtains". In all three cases, the context prompted the association with lacemaking. But the very different sensibilities of the three architects suggest that there is more to the convergence between the art of thread and that of architecture than a mere coincidence.

In Nottingham, Caruso St John chose an edging pattern from the large collection of lace of the local university (typically, lacemaking is limited by its technique to a width of 120 mm) that suited the vertical scalloped panels of their project. They desired a faithful, rather than "pop" reproduction of the motif. The lace was scanned to make a three-dimensional computer model. This model was translated with a CNC milling machine into an MDF positive, and an 11-metre-long rubber mould was made, suitable for casting in reinforced concrete. The immensely fine pattern, consisting of a mesh with naturalist fillings, will be "like plants or frost" climbing up the fluted surface of

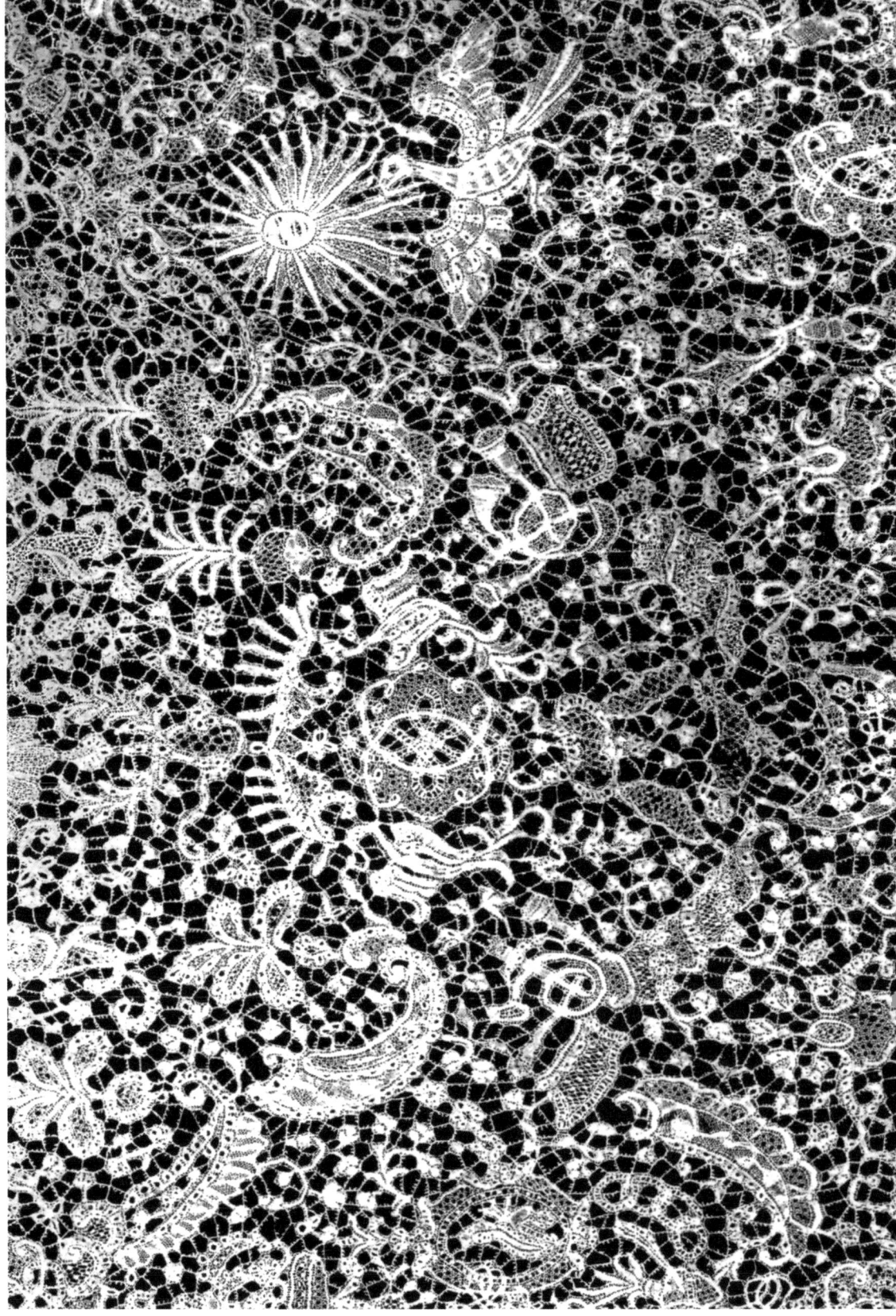

immensely tall concrete panels. Not unlike the hopvine, perhaps, climbing on the colossal, fractured trunk of a birch likened by Gogol to a column of marble.

In Leicester, FOA presented images of lace at the competition stage. They later selected a fabric pattern from the John Lewis archive and adapted it to suit specific functional purposes. To increase the transparency of the curtain wall, they omitted a secondary layer of curlicues. The scale and position of the remaining arabesque was adjusted so that a person's face might occasionally coincide with the curves of tendrils and afford unobstructed views. In places, stems were thickened to limit solar gain. Consisting of two skins with a gap in between for maintenance, the ceramic frit on the inner skin of the curtain wall is reflected in the mirror frit on the outer skin, causing the pattern to become denser, to grow and to lose itself. In this way, ornament and mirrors – both of them loved by the rococo – are combined in a single arrangement. The effect is one of extraordinary confusion, the arabesque becoming somewhat immaterial in a play that involves, like the eighteenth-century theatre of Marivaux, reflection, illusion and *double-entendre*.

In Nottingham, a clear distinction is maintained between the surface ornament and the architectonic order of the fluted panels. In Leicester, by contrast, this distinction is minimised: the ornament is simultaneously functional and decorative; in a literal and metaphorical sense, the ornament is given depth. In both instances, however, the ornament is sober, delicate and complex, and the architects clearly took pleasure in something akin to "the indistinct play of little forms full of vivacity" that has been attributed to lace.

This is precisely the kind of aesthetic sensation described by Benoit Mendelbrot, the inventor of fractal geometry. In a little-known article on architecture (surely one of the very few written by a mathematician), Mendelbrot distinguishes between scalebound objects, in which characteristics of scale, such as length and width, are few in number, each having a distinct size, from scaling objects, objects in which very many different elements of any imaginable size are present. In scaling objects, "there are," he writes, "so many different scales, and their harmonics are so interlaced and interact so confusingly that they are not really distinct from each other, but merge into a continuum."

Among examples of scalebound objects, he mentions the spherical radomes of Buckminster Fuller and "Bauhaus style, glass cube-type buildings". Among scaling objects, besides mountains, lakes and sea coasts of which, famously, he made computer models, he mentions Garnier's Opera House in Paris (the article was written in 1978, two years after the show on the Ecole des Beaux Arts at MOMA in New York). Today, in spite of the brevity of the *beaux-arts* revival, the choice of example remains interesting insofar as the ornament (as opposed to the composition) of the Paris Opera House continues to elicit the same distaste. Yet, in the eyes of Mendelbrot, its ornament represents what he calls "an aesthetic of scale". Scaling objects, he argues, can be interesting or trivial, depending on the distance from which an object is being observed, and on the formal variety offered within one's frame of vision.

Few people are better trained to discern such variety than lace-makers, the creators of "little forms full of vivacity". Like scaling objects, lace exhibits many different scales that come in and out of focus, depending upon one's attention. Its *ground* or *network* consists of units that can be round, square or hexagonal, made with the looping, plaiting and twisting of threads. It is sometimes scattered with *leaves* (decorative stitches resembling grains of wheat), or covered with *neige* (a secondary ground of spots resembling snow). On the basis of this, ornamental motifs or *fillings* appear that are distinct from the motifs of the design proper. The warp and weft of the lace are built at the same time (this distinguishes lace from weaving and places no limit upon design) in a virtuoso play which not even lacemakers can analyse. This virtuosity fuses a multiplicity of scales and confuses a multiplicity of motifs. It also tends towards the infinitely small, to a degree that ruined the eyes of lacemakers almost as surely as the art of miniature. Like Impressionism, had it been bleached and deprived of its subjects, for lace digests all motifs, be they abstract or figurative, inside the manifold of its texture.

Likewise, there is in contemporary architecture a marked interest in texture: in the impression made upon the eye by the intricacy of patterns and the tactile surface of materials. But it is difficult not to feel that our time, as Loos said of his own exactly one hundred years ago, has yet to produce its own ornament. Architects borrow, copy, enlarge and adapt existing patterns. Occasionally, artists are commissioned on their behalf, the art of decoration having replaced the decorative arts. In this, Herzog & de Meuron showed the way. But curiosity can seem directed more towards the process of reproduction than to the ornament itself. William Morris, Louis Sullivan and the Papuans designed their own ornament; we don't.

More fundamentally, the emotive quality of ornament is now so reduced as to seem redundant. The modern movement insisted that beauty needed no ornament: beauty was to follow from the correct handling of material and function. Beauty, however, proved natural neither to the building of infrastructures nor to commercial construction, and the aesthetic reality of modernity turned out to be a disappointment. Beauty collects instead in the reservations of historical cities. It survives in accessories to the financial compositions of commercial development: in the icons that sometimes embellish our skylines and in luxurious claddings pinned onto the tight corset of regulations. No longer the attribute of the erotic and the sacred, ornament grows in inverse proportion to the fading of beauty. What it loses in charm, it gains in pathos.

Peter Ward-Jackson, Rococo Ornament: a History in Pictures, V & A, 1984.
Marie Risselin-Steenebrugen, Trois siècles de dentelles aux Musées royaux d'Art et d'Histoire. 1980
Neutelings Riedijk, At Work, 2004.
For a development of the argument, see The Function of Ornament, edited by Farshid Moussavi and Michael Kubo, 2006.
Idem note ii. Benoit B. Mendelbrot, "Scalebound or scaling shapes: A Useful distinction in the visual arts and in the natural sciences", in Leonardo, Vol. 14, pp. 54–47, 1981.

An example of Brussels bobbin lace from the Musées Royaux d'Art et d'Histoire, dated 1708, Image from Marie Risselin-Steenebrugen's book Trois siècles de dentelles aux Musées Royaux d'Art et d'Histoire (1980).

Photography

By Maria Lantz
Photographer and teacher, Sweden

Photography and architecture have been closely linked ever since the infancy of photography. Like dancing partners, playmates or antagonistic rivals, the two disciplines are involved in a virtuoso interplay. Their interdependence and their anthropophagous devouring of each other are an ever-recurrent ritual. But photography and architecture are not only tied together. Like sworn criminal accomplices they are also united in their offensiveness to other disciplines. The "crime" consists in their impurity, their unwillingness to be one thing or the other. Neither art nor utility. Neither technique nor aesthetic. Neither science nor poetry. Or rather, all of these things at once: utility, aesthetic, technique and poetry!

Cameras existed long before the invention of photography. The very earliest, known probably for millennia, were rooms, at one time perhaps caves, in which special phenomena of light were observable. A dark room with a small circular aperture could under certain conditions, when the light was refracted through the opening, display the outside world as a projection – upside down – on the opposite wall. What magic! These first cameras were called *camera obscura* – Latin for "dark room".

It is remarkable how closely the etymology of the camera is connected to words signifying home and architecture. The very basis of the camera, the box without its lens, is called the camera *body* in English, but in Swedish the camera "house" – *kamerahus*. And the lens attached to the camera is likened to the eye: the vision or gaze of the camera, attached to a body or a house. And houses too are said to have eyes – *vinduer* in several Nordic languages, becoming *window* in English: "wind eye". Body and house and eye.

Eventually the camera obscura was to evolve into photography as we know it. This was achieved with lenses and glass projection surfaces, but the actual photograph, the "light script", was not born until the evanescent projection could be permanently secured without a human hand drawing what was made manifest. This happened in about the 1830s, when it was discovered how silver salts reacted when exposed to light, a chemical discovery of decisive consequence for vision and memory. Now, for the first time ever, photography could be used to show what something had looked like in another place, at another point in time.

If the first cameras can be described as rooms, the first photographic images are photographs taken looking out of rooms, telling us of prospects and – architecture. Daguerre's famous view of Paris, in which he chanced to capture a shoeshine man and his customer, shows a city under construction, with rows of newly planted trees lining a Haussmann Boulevard in the making. Niépce picture of a country estate shows a different view, with sun and shadow outlining the architecture, coarse-grained, to the point of abstraction.

Architectural photographs aestheticise and present; they make it possible to move, reduce and reproduce architecture, time and place. They reduce and frame. By means of the photograph, a place or an object is elevated to something valuable, something worth looking at. As soon as photographs became available and printable, the photograph became a tool of the architect's profession. The photograph showed that a building was built, that it was chosen, and knowledge of this could be rapidly spread all over the world through magazines and posters. For the first time the picture in itself could constitute the distinction between the notional and the accomplished.

And yet there is something odd about architecture allowing itself to be photographed in the first place. For it is indeed strange that architecture, the most three-dimensional thing people have learned to create, something which humans make for themselves but which cannot be moved, cannot be understood in a moment, has an outside and an inside, a topside and underside, this unique phenomenon, has been a subject of photography ever since the camera was born. Yet photographs are two-dimensional. They are small and flat! Photographs can be mass-produced and moved about, they are object and fragment. How can it be that architectural photographs have become so important for the understanding and appraisal of architecture?

In *Private and Public*, Beatriz Colomina argues that it is the media, their photographs included, that make modern architecture modern. We cannot therefore speak of the architecture of modernism without also including photographs, printing technology and consumption. Communication via the media is the foundation of modern humanity, of capitalism and knowledge transmission, and photography plays a decisive role in all this, both for the spreading of architectural ideas and for the view taken of the world generally.

The invention of photography is usually seen in connection with other nineteenth-century inventions such as the telegraph and the railway. But we have to remember that photography is also a question of magic, of the inherently supernatural. The magic of photography is due to the apparent possibility of being in two places at once, or at different points in time simultaneously. This is fundamentally unnatural, or even supernatural. And the supernatural, that which turns our senses upside down and surprises us to such a degree that we can longer be sure of what is true and what is invention, dream or reality, is basically frightening. During the infancy of photography this was obvious. Photographers really *were* magical and unintelligible, spooky. And for that very reason also titillating, wonderful and fantastic! The phenomenon can, if you like, be described in grammatical terms: through photography and the imperfect, a *then*, is transferred to a *here and now*. We can speak of an overturning of tenses, which is basically what photography is all about. The instant this happens, the picture becomes proof of what once happened. The photograph as an indexical sign, that is to say, something pointing back towards what previously caused it, like the footprint in the sand. Except that it also pictures what it is referring to. The photograph unites magic and science. And this, although we have nearly forgotten it, remains the rare attractive force of photography and its entirely unique competence.

Photographs quickly became popular artefacts, the uses of which ranged from high to low in all strata of society – from scientific expeditions to visiting card photography, from artistic *mise-en-scène* to pornography, from criminological surveys to documentations of war. Photographs became decorations, they were displayed, sold as picture postcards, as art or as collectables. Illustrated magazines and amateur photography followed in due course. The fact that photographs attracted contemporary beholders in the first half of the twentieth century to such a degree that they also became a species of architectural element is a point Beatriz Colomina raises when describing Le Corbusier and the picture window. With the picture window, she maintains, the view becomes furnishing, a decorative picture on which to gaze securely, like a photograph. But let us invert the perspective. When one stands in front of a building with picture windows, especially in the evening and with the inside lit up, the private becomes visible, inside becomes outside. The window picture also becomes the view inwards, insight into the private sphere. Making the private public is also in keeping with what photography has been doing, above all since the 1920s, when the miniature camera was developed and indoor photography became possible. This development was quickly followed by an explosion of pictures showing the private sphere, pictures printed in magazines such as *Time, Life* and (in Sweden) *Bild* and *Se*. These magazines were hugely popular, offering features from every corner of the world, about the celebrities, film

stars and politicians of the time, as well as feature articles about "ordinary people". The private became idealised and was looked on as interesting. With the aid of photography, private and public begin to change places. The private is made public and the public – media – is consumed in the private sphere.

And that is where we stand today. Consumption of pictures has hardly diminished. Instead, picture production in this digital age is greater than at any other time in human history. How many photographs do we see in a day? Thousands?

We appear to acquiesce to this superabundance, we live in a pictorial culture where pictures are our common references. For the photograph has replaced private memory and relieved the visual gaze – emancipated it, possibly. Vision is no longer needed in order to gather information; the camera does that. Instead we can use our gaze for enjoyment, as Richard Crary puts it.

Scophophilia, the pleasure of looking, is ever-present in our age. If Le Corbusier introduced the picture window as the architectural projection screen for the view outwards and also for looking in, today this is, if anything, a rule of architecture. Dark scenes have become our new taboo and have yielded to interiors in buildings where the window has vanished and been succeeded by glass walls. At the same time the transparent building can be see as a panopticon, a Benthamite prison, but a prison in which we have learned to like the supervisory gaze. An exhibitionism and a voyeurism in which architecture and photography are both a means and an end. It is no longer the world that is projected into the home but the home that is hung out, picture-like, in the world at large.

The dark room, the camera obscura, has been turned inside out and the room has become a projection, a picture, a photograph.

Andreas Gursky, Copan, 2002. C-print mounted on plexiglas in artist's frame 81 x 103 inches; 206 x 262 cm. Copyright Andreas Gursky, courtesy Matthew Marks Gallery, New York.

Slit

By Johan Linton
Architect and civil engineer, Sweden

Architecture embodies diversity, a complex structure of elements with superimposed meanings in which archaic origin and individual narratives run intertwined through the history of building. Even ostensibly simple elements are recreated or bifurcate in constantly new connections and through new interpretations. And so the proper definition of such an open architectural phenomenon as the slit or incision is not altogether clear. This, then, is hardly an account but rather a narrative, a free gesture cutting incompletely through an extensive kaleidoscopic field.

Early on, the slit had a place in the architecture of fortification. The wall, the tower, the breast wall, were given small apertures – tall, slit-like loopholes. These were defensive installations aimed from the inside outwards. A narrow incision in the structure made it possible to safely survey and act in the neighbouring space without having to expose oneself to it. Apertures which created a bipolar relation between two adjacent rooms. The almost inverted difference between two such spatialities is effectively illustrated by Castel del Monte, where the fine, precise incisions contrast with the huge and geometrically monumental masonry standing out against the landscape. There the contrast between "within" and "without" is dramatic. Something similar can be said about the moat – a deep ditch accentuating the already asymmetrical relation between two spatial zones. The difference between the fortification or barrier and the space beyond is further reinforced. Even though instances of this kind refer primarily to the art of fortification, the possibility that other aspects also have an influence on the making of them cannot be discounted. The slit, like any other element of architecture, is open to aesthetic values – a conditioning factor which always diverts and fragments the purely pragmatic, functional approaches.

Throughout history one can also distinguish small apertures of this kind which may have had other spatial implications. The window openings of Romanesque churches are sometimes of slit-like narrowness and positioned in a way suggesting that they were of importance for the atmosphere and character of the room, rather than serving any fortificatory purpose. In such cases the slit is placed in a more articulate relation to the window – an excision more intended to open up the connection between two spatial contexts. Both these apertures are in a sense bipolar, but the slit establishes a more drastic asymmetry. The slit connects, though without opening up.

What can be said, then, about the effect of the slit? The slit unites two rooms, albeit without opening them up to each other. Aside from fine daylight openings or lookout points, the soft-spoken presence of one room and another can be regarded as a kind of effect in itself. Perhaps the phenomenon can be best observed in the slashed canvases of Lucio Fontana. They present not just a dash over a surface but an incision in which three-dimensional movements occur surrounding the narrow line; a spatial tension field. Often, though not always, this effect differs in character on the two sides of the slit. In the case of Fontana's art, which is a kind of illustration of the effect of the slit, there are also references from buildings, such as the copper-sheathed signal box by Herzog & de Meuron, in which the slashed "canvas" has been translated into a volume. At the same time the slit, like the window, reveals something about the building component or building material which it pierces. Wall thicknesses and surfaces are articulated in the room.

With Modernism, something of the idea of the window has been successfully realised in a previously unknown manner, it has become technically possible for the façade of the building to be made entirely of glass. At the same time the slit has come to be increasingly used in architecture. The principle of the aperture has been explored in the direction of both convergence and divergence. Even in modern architecture the slit has been used functionally, pragmatically, to admit a limited amount of light – both into rooms which do not have enough space for big windows and in larger rooms which had to be protected from people looking in, or from excessive light. In this way the slit recurs in the early buildings and projects of Modernism. Already in the model of Maison Citrohan, presented at Salon d'Automne in 1922, Le Corbusier contrasted both large continuous areas of fenestration and ribbon windows with narrow incisions or slits. The relatively pragmatic use of the slit in this particular instance later came to be developed and varied in the direction of the suggestive and enigmatic, as in the use of slit-like elements in a buildings like Ronchamp and La Tourette. The same kind of pragmatic and aesthetic use of the slit recurs in the works of a host of other modern architects, such as Frank Lloyd Wright, Louis Kahn and Mario Botta. In a work like the funeral monument for the Brion family, Carlo Scarpa displays a whole range of variations on the motif and thematic potential of the slit.

An almost playful application of how slit and wall can be integrated is Herzog & de Meuron's undulating shutter façade in Schützenmattstrasse in Basel. The narrow façade also demonstrates how the infill project in general can be regarded as a situation where slit and building interact.

In the many contemporary breaches with traditionalism in architecture, as supported by new building technology, the slit has come to be used in other ways as well. Architects like Daniel Libeskind and Peter Eisenman allow narrow apertures to occur as a consequence of the architecture being subjected to abstract, predetermined systems projecting sections through the building. Perhaps one of the most widely noted examples is Libeskind's Jewish Museum in Berlin, a building whose interior and exterior both expressively accentuate the presence of the slit. Through the expressive incisions in both façade and interior, with those in the latter exposing inaccessible slit-like rooms, the building has been intertwined with the slit. If the slit was formerly dictated by the structure of the building, now it is the structure which has to defer to the incision. Another building in which the slit plays an important role is Eisenman's *House VI*, in which orthogonal sections – as in Libeskind's building – no longer act discreetly in the background but take possession of the dwelling – and with it of man's most intimate spaces – by cutting up its walls, floor and ceiling. In such instances the slit can, somewhat remotely, put one in mind of Beaux Arts architecture, where elements of form are transferred to the building from the outside.

If, finally, we permit ourselves to contemplate just individual aspects of the character and properties of the slit, perhaps it is not entirely groundless to mention, for example, an architecture like Filippo Brunelleschi's. The precise play of grey rib-like elements on abstract pale surfaces can be regarded as a kind of negative use of the slit, but which nevertheless has a kindred effect. This kind of view seems to be corroborated, for example, by the tall, slit-like windows of a building like Santo Spirito.

This scanty selection of examples from different historical and cultural contexts is in itself sufficient to hint at an elusive diversity, a diversification of applications and interpretations which, even in a more exhaustive and methodical account, is liable to stray through the shifts and crevices which inevitably occur in the structure of the narrative.

Andres Serrano. The Morgue (Rat Poison Suicide II), 1992. Copyright A. Serrano. Printed by courtesy of the artist and the Paula Cooper Gallery, New York.

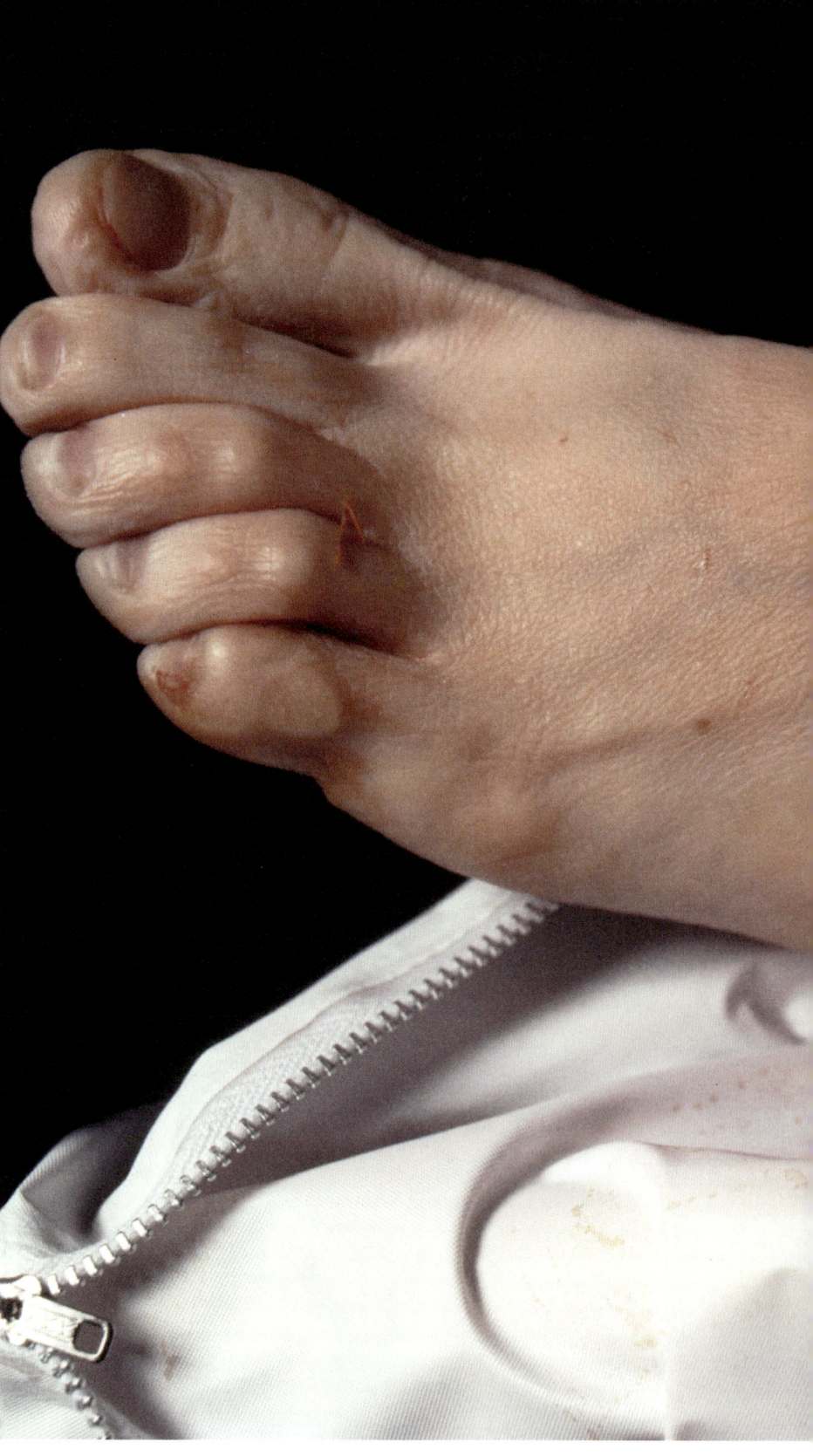

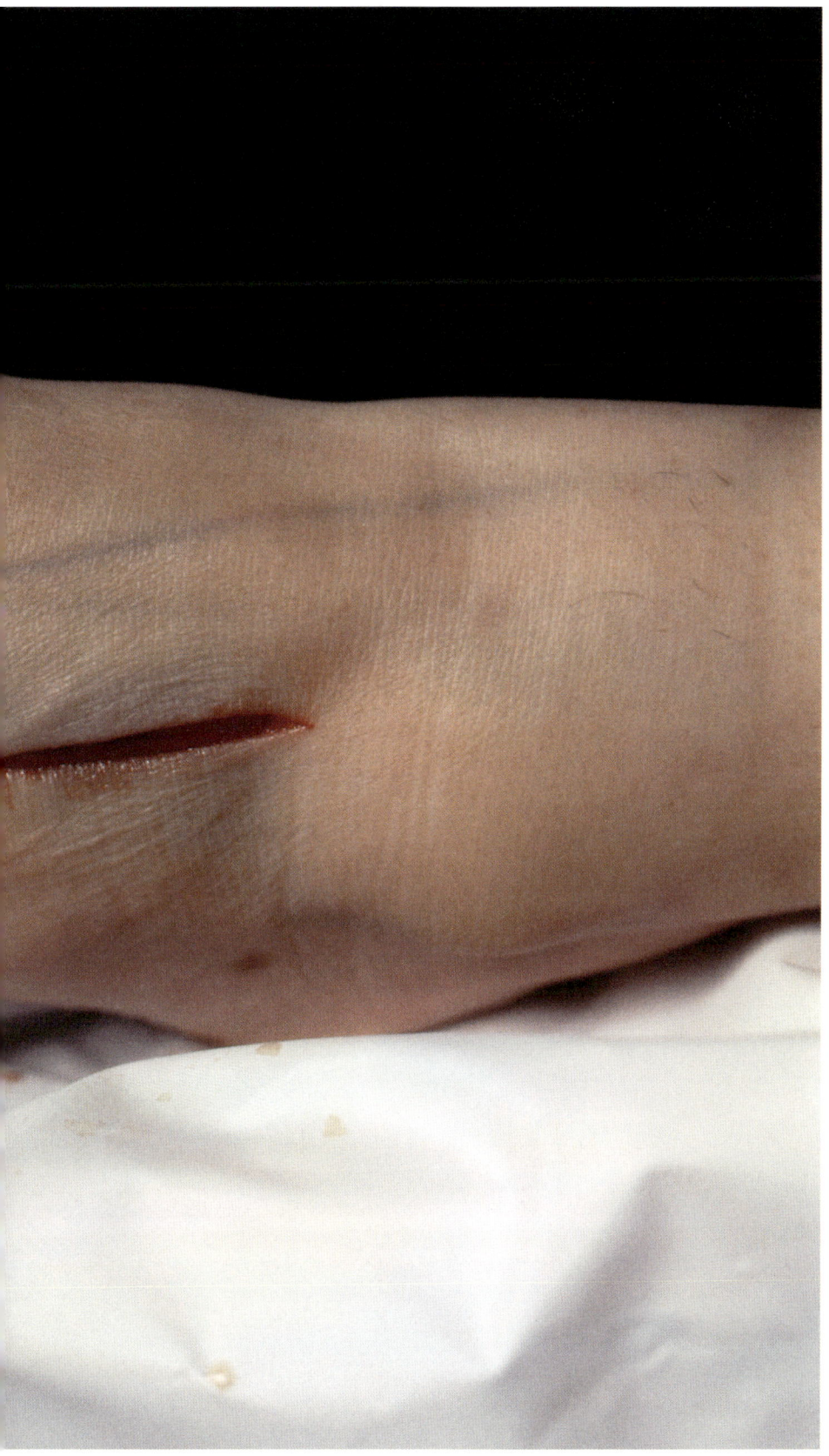

Technology

By Joseph Rykwert
Professor Emeritus of Architecture at the University
of Pennsylvania, USA and UK

Techné is the Greek word for any skilled making; hence *technikos*, a skilled maker or craftsman (and *archi-technikos* is the chief craftsman); from it most European languages derive "technique", the word for a learned skill. The suffix "-logy" is from the Greek *logos*: a momentous "word" which could also mean "discourse" - or even "method".

No building can be built without some technique. The most various building animals – beavers and bower-birds, termites and sticklebacks – acquire building instincts in the course of evolutionary differentiation. Only humans have technology, which is an aptitude to reason about technique, to modify and improve it.

The word itself is recent in modern languages. "Technology" was imported into English from the French late in the eighteenth century when the suffix *-logie* was added to all sorts of terms. Of course the first of all the *-logies*, Theology, was a notion and a word known to both Plato and Aristotle. It was Aristotle who actually coined the word "technology" when he investigated the rules governing the technique of persuasive discourse which he termed rhetoric. Astrology and later Geology followed. Yet even the words "technique", "technic" do not appear commonly in European languages until the eighteenth century.

And yet the skills required for building must be as old as any building procedures. Greek words derived from *tech, *tek originally referred to carpentry – perhaps by imitating the knocking of hammers and axes, but they came to be used of craft in general, perhaps because they also related to the many words to do with weaving whose root, *tex has never been disentangled by philologists from the woodworking *tek. Nineteenth-century historians proposed weaving as the original craft, and the earliest surviving human habitations already display a refined variety of such aptitudes: the huts of skin, branches and animal bones in the northern valleys of the Dniester and the Rhine are dated to the old stone age – somewhere between 30,000 and 20,000 BC – and they already show the skills of lashing pieces of wood or large bones together, as well as a knowledge of skin-curing and sewing. All this suggests that these builders had ambitions (which some animals developed earlier) to make their dwellings showy: mammoth tusks are used to frame entrances and weigh down the leather flaps of their tents. This should not be surprising: these builders are roughly contemporary with cave-painters in Western Europe, of whose dwellings we know pitifully little.

A spurt in building techniques coincided with the beginnings of agriculture in the fertile crescent; as the cultivation and breeding of grasses and animals began, new kinds of shelter were devised which used wood and dried grass, but also clay and mud clods, sun-dried long before there was any thought of baking them. We do not know when the first notions of rendering such walls with a slurry – watered mud (or even diluted cow dung) – first appeared, nor when these dwellings were first grouped into articulated settlements. Such grouping may, indeed, be earlier and quite separate from the growth of building techniques. At any rate, by the time the first "urban" settlement that we know of, old Jericho, was built (before 9,000 BC), a chalky slurry was being used to secure mud brick walls and was even moulded into faces over skulls for funerary rites. To the north-west, in southern Anatolia, Çatal Hüyuk and Haçilar already show elaborate rendering techniques to provide a ground for painted and moulded ornament, some of it incorporating animal remains – especially skulls and horns. The documented persistence of techniques and even forms over generations shows that such peoples had transmittable and learnable technologies.

Building tools were also perfected. The axe, which may have been a weapon before it was a tool, is differentiated during the neolithic period into the adze (*Erminette, Krummaxt*), a blade fixed with the edge at right-angle to the handle, the ancestor of the modern plane. In the dense forests of northern Europe stone axes were used to clear, slash and burn clearings, but also to fashion the first wooden huts. In a moist northern climate wood does not have the staying power of even the most friable of bricks in the fertile crescent, so we know more about the development of stone axes than about the buildings which they fashioned.

Brick and ceramic building techniques were Mesopotamian, while stone ones were first developed on the Iranian plateau and in Egypt; they were inherited by the Greeks and modified by the Romans, who also devised ambitious brick vaulting. The tensile strength of timber was appreciated by most brick and stone builders – hence the millenary export value of "the cedars of Lebanon". Yet in some parts of the world – in Mesoamerica, and in the Indian sub-continent – large-stone building was not sophisticated by any similar coupling of compressive with tensile elements.

European builders of the Middle Ages developed different stone vaulting forms, using small stones that had been shaped through elaborate geometrical cutting techniques, while their cunning use of buttressing and counterbalance to free large areas of wall from structural use prompted the growth of novel glass technologies. All such techniques were taken up by western and southern European sixteenth- and seventeenth-century builders, while analogous timber building methods were developed in northern Europe and across the Eurasian steppes, and became most highly refined in Eastern Asia.

In the second half of the eighteenth century, the development of many technologies was speeded up by the industrializing of metal (cast iron and later steel), as well as of glass production, and the combining of tensile reinforcement with inert material – cement concrete (known since antiquity), as well as new sources of energy. The increasing mathematical skills these demanded led to the formation of a new profession – that of the engineer (from the late Latin *ingenium*, a siege-machine), which was fostered in the new Polytechnic schools (Paris 1794, Vienna 1815, Karlsruhe 1825, Dresden 1838, Zurich 1853). That new profession also provided architects with technical support, though it outgrew that role so that much industrial building was done without the benefit of architectural input. Towards the end of the nineteenth century, high building stretched the resources of existing technologies. Advances – such as the structural use of glass – grew exponentially during the twentieth century, and their refinements came to be known as "high technology", the enthusiasm for which, in its last decades, led to the formation of a dominant, very linear manner or style nicknamed "high-tech". It was characterized by an emphatic treatment of technical devices such as structural cabling which becomes an ornamental feature, while the metal and glass surfaces the style favoured were otherwise exceedingly plain. By the beginning of the twenty-first century, this has been replaced by a manner in which the technological achievements, though still on the whole "high", have assumed the arbitrary and extravagant shapes which the advances in technology have now allowed and/or stimulated.

At the end of the twentieth century and in the first years of the twenty-first century, a great change came over the drafting office rather than the building site which was due to the impact of information technology. Though it called on the structural achievements of high-tech, computer drafting seems to have liberated designers from the orthogonal nature of construction, and allowed the arbitrary and extravagant shapes which such advances in technology have stimulated.

Honeycomb. Copyright Scanpix/Corbis.

Tradition

By Vittorio Magnago Lampugnani
Architect and Professor of the History of Urban Design at
the ETH Zurich, Switzerland.

Nowadays to describe designs for cities, architecture or commodities as innovative is equivalent to paying them a compliment. The novelty of a work compared to its predecessors, whatever it happens to be, is considered a quality.

This has not always been so. Newness as a merit in itself is a discovery of romantic art criticism. Until the second half of the eighteenth century, the categories of judgement were harmony, completeness, balance, perfection. With the advent of Romanticism the situation was reversed: the categories suddenly became dissonance, the non-finished, surprise. And, above all, innovation.

This goes for all artistic forms and has remained so almost without exception until today – even for those art forms most tied to concrete necessities, such as urban planning and architecture. Their recent historiography has inculcated in us the image of an uninterrupted sequence of experiments whose interest is directly proportional to their eye-catching appeal; as if the most startling, incredible and weird designs were somehow automatically the most worthy of attention and applause.

Doubts about this sort of judgement structure have put orthodox art criticism and production in a crisis. Several variously agreeable though always unconvincing revivals have ensued. Underlying them perhaps has been the assumption that design is at best a work of art and, at worst, an exercise of style.

If we look instead at design as a craft, the classes of value operate on a completely different level: that of appropriateness. Craft does not require (and does not tolerate) experimentalism; it needs to construct for itself, work by work, a firm foundation of rules and wisdom. It never allows abrupt change, but necessitates continuity.

It does however allow adjustment, modification, slight improvement. No craft is a closed entity formed by laws laid down once and for all: otherwise it would be a dead craft. Design, too, is constantly evolving. Every new work widens its disciplinary corpus, reforms its rules and widens its horizon.

At first sight, this may seem too little. Our eyes, accustomed by now to the rude upheavals perpetrated by avant-gardes, have lost their capacity to observe minimal changes and imperceptible differences. But it is on these minimal changes, these imperceptible differences, that for tens, hundreds and thousands of years the history of urban planning and architecture has been built. Roman architecture is profoundly different from Greek architecture; but the external symptoms on which that difference rests are exiguous indeed. Renaissance design culture is quite different from that of the ancient world; yet they both use the same formal elements in compositions that rely on the same grammars. The history of cities, houses and things was, until the late eighteenth century, built upon a constantly but very delicately, almost invisibly renovated continuity. Thereafter changes occurred more rapidly and more incisively, until they tore disciplines to pieces in the tumult of the first half of last century.

This process is irreversible but also, we believe, over. All imaginable heresies have been committed. They cannot be ignored, nor can they be superseded; at the most, they may be repeated. However, a whim fired off for the second or third time will be a damp squib; permanent transgression ends up becoming the rule. It only remains to consider even the avant-gardes a period of history which belongs to the past. And to start looking at the present again not as an autonomous phase, detached from evolution by a revolutionary outburst, but as an integral part of a tradition to be rediscovered and reappropriated.

This, of course, does not mean taking a step backwards. As noted above, the process of change in history is irreversible. The question is, on the contrary, to appraise the situation in a given period and turn it to advantage.

Since the forgoing of novelty at all costs undoubtedly is of advantage to design, it need no longer cling to the meagre support of an individual's momentary intuition, but can lean instead on the solid foundations of a collective endeavour built up and proven over time. This requires commitment. Tradition is not hereditary, like nobility; it is earned by study and work. But only from tradition can objects, buildings and cities be born with the quality of durability. Only on the strength of tradition, beyond all superficial formalism, can an authentic style be crystallized. In short, only the power of tradition can take up the challenges of an epoch afflicted by the tedium of excessive image-consumption and devoted to parsimony.

Paul Valéry, on the subject of his own work, wrote candidly: "... I do not have the superstition of use. I consider my archaisms innovations, which may or may not establish themselves, depending on the advantages of use and on the energy of action and the field". And he was echoed by his contemporary and friend Auguste Perret: "He who, without betraying modern materials or programmes, produces a work that seems always to have existed and is, in a word, ordinary, may consider himself satisfied".

Let us follow the French poet's and architect's exhortation. Let us adopt traditional forms wherever we feel they are right and appropriate. Let us try, without overlooking the programmes imposed upon us by our condition as contemporaries, to produce works that look as if they had always been there. Let us avoid useless inventions, gratuitous changes. Let us not be afraid of the commonplace but sharpen our sensitivity towards its hidden elegance. Let us opt, where necessary, for subtle innovation.

The chief concern of last century's architectural avant-garde was to be modern. Everyone and everything had to be able to flaunt the attribute and boast its characteristic: material, technique, working method, and even style, art and life. From futurism onwards, the programmes and manifestos of planners, architects, craft and industrial designers never stopped repeating, at least till the 'seventies, their obsession with form but also with content.

Without ever looking into its deeper meaning. Originally the term "modern" stood, in a rather sibylline way, for "what is ours, now"; and this etymology was more than sufficient for its purpose. Because the purpose was to break away sharply from the past and project itself triumphantly, all purged and renewed, into the present if not even into the future.

At least in theory. The avant-gardist programme never really came into effect in design or still less in its realization. Particularly symptomatic is the role of technology in architecture during the 1920s. There was a lot of talk about industrialized building, new modes of construction and "modern" technologies. With very few exceptions however, houses continued to be built with bricks and mortar, and were at once modestly concealed beneath a thin layer of fragile white plaster. The plaster, along with one or two other formal features – the flat roof, the ribbon windows, the stilts, the iron railing of nautical origin – certified its modern quality.

Design culture, though caught in the furore of modernism, had almost always been stranded in modernist formalism, which immediately became a kind of exclusive club. Those who espoused its idiom and metaphors were members, the others were barred. This curious discrimination produced as many equally odd classifications, aided by a glaringly partisan historiography to this day in vogue, according to which Giuseppe Terragni was a modern architect and Marcello

Piacentini a non-modern, and so on: Adalberto Libera yes and Giovanni Muzio no; Ludwig Mies van der Rohe yes and Heinrich Tessenow no; Le Corbusier yes and Fernand Pouillon no.

Now we know, of course, that this game of "goodies and baddies" is ridiculous and that all these architects were modern architects: because they all worked in a mass society, in a highly industrialized world and in a anti-historicist culture. We know very well, but we get scant satisfaction from it. Because today we do not care whether we are modern or not.

We want to carry on our architectural work as a craft. And in terms of craft, the concept of modernity makes no sense at all.

The concept of modernity implies a break, a breach from what is not "now", "not ours". But in our craft, no such breach exists. The present is indissolubly tied to the past, and is part and parcel of more than three thousand years of history as far as architecture and urban planning are concerned; and as a collective work constructed in time, in some way it is all "ours". Tradition is an indivisible part of our working experience and as such it belongs to us.

Our masters, our examples to be emulated, and our travelling companions, can be chosen at random from among our contemporaries or from the past. "Every man", wrote Henri Focillon, "is first of all contemporary to himself and his generation, but he is also contemporary to the spiritual group of which he is a part. The artist is even more so, because these ancestors and friends are for him not memories but a presence. They stand before him, more alive than ever".

We are not artists, only artisans; but for us too, these ancestors and friends are alive and present. They are naturally those who practised the same craft as ours and on the same principles. But they are also philosophers, men and women of letters, painters and sculptors who, in different and sometimes obscure ways, contributed to the construction of a disciplinary corpus apparently extraneous to them. Our masters are therefore certainly those of the so-called Modern Movement; but also, and perhaps still more, Hippodamos of Miletus, Filippo Brunelleschi, Donato Bramante, Baldassarre Peruzzi, Etienne-Louis Boullée, Karl Friedrich Schinkel. They are Giotto, Piero della Francesca, Andrea Mantegna, Ingres, Paul Cézanne. They are Dante Alighieri, William Shakespeare, Gustave Flaubert, Robert Musil. They are Giovanni Battista Vico and Immanuel Kant.

At times we learn more from artists like Brunelleschi or Piero, because they faced and solved problems that are also ours, in an incomparably timely and precise way. They are giants of their craft and art. However Schinkel and Musil are, despite this, closer: because the conditions of their work are more similar to ours.

So we discover that we are, almost despite ourselves, irremediably modern. For modernity is not modernism; it is not a choice of style, it is a condition. Those working today as architects acting in good conscience as contemporaries, cannot evade that condition. Their craft, if practised well and seriously, is indissolubly bound up with life, and their works will necessarily respect the period in which they took shape. They cannot ignore this in order to pursue phantoms extraneous to their time. They cannot indulge in passing fashions. In short, they cannot impose themselves as individuals upon the culture in which they operate and which, even if subversively, they are bound to interpret.

This culture is, for us, ineluctably, that of the modern.

Transformation

By Mikael Bergquist
Architect and writer, Sweden

First, two short digressions, one about jazz and one about clothing, which I encountered recently and which, although they have nothing whatsoever to do with architecture, curiously touch on the theme of this text. The American art critic Dave Hickey writes of his favourite record, *Chet Baker Sings*: "I played it all the time, morning and night, and it spoke to me then of a special kind of elegiac cool; it dispensed with all pretension to musical heroism without repudiating the idea of heroism itself." In the record, which was made at the end of the 1950s, Baker sings American jazz standards. His performance is entirely free from the critics' cult of "originality" and masculine "self-expression". Chet Baker plays and sings the songs without any vibrato, "bel canto" or "powerful" statements. "In contemporary terms," Hickey writes, "Baker does not so much 'perform' these songs as 'simulate' them – appropriating their complete content to his own intentions while leaving the song itself with its formal integrity unmolested."

An amusing article in the magazine *Fantastic Man* about the French article Benoît Duteurtre describes the French *style Négligé* mode of dress. A French mix of good taste, quality wear, shabbiness and appropriate unfashionability. Deliberate unawareness of dress. "*style négligé* (not to be confused with the American 'casual style') exists neither in Anglo-Saxon countries, where people think that clothing is an unambiguous language of the market, nor in wholly Latin countries, which find their rhetoric in the perfection of exaggeration. No one can teach it, because each of its strategies is personal, and also because those who practice it refuse to admit they do."

In a section of the book *Progetto e utopia* Manfredo Tafuri argues, concerning experimental architecture, that avant-garde movements, whether eighteenth-century revolutionary architecture or twentieth-century Modernism, are exclusive and absolutist. They do not reason unnecessarily with the reality they are rejecting. They aspire to build a wholly new world. Experimental architecture, on the other hand, makes use of slight shifts and disruptions within the given code. It lacks a centre, is self-contradictory, speaks many languages at once and presents conflicting images. This is a radical and telling criticism of avant-garde myths, value systems and methods, Tafuri writes. Experimental architecture in the form of late classical antiquity, stone Gothic, Mannerism, and the experimentalism of the eighteenth century and modernism, exists in the struggle against the established languages, but its true purpose is not to bring about a complete revolution; instead the most positive results of an experimental attitude are the cracks and explosive charges introduced in the contemporary code. Often, like time bombs, they will explode at some future date. The architectural work acquires the form of a question, not a statement. A subversive transformation from within.

Example 1:

In the mid-eighteenth century the architect Giovanni Battista Piranesi created a series of etchings which he entitled *Carceri d'Inventione*, "imaginary prisons". In its second and final form the series comprises sixteen sheets, enigmatic images in which we encounter a seemingly endless subterranean, labyrinthine prison world. Steps lead to landings which lead to new steps and new landings *ad infinitum*. What we are looking into is not the geometrically defined spaces of classicism. The diversity, distortions and disintegration of these pictures are in fact a systematic critique of the idea of a centre.

A reconstruction of Piranesi's perspective on one level, insofar as it is possible, shows that the complex building structures originate in random sequences of rooms. We also find that Piranesi has undermined the laws of perspective by using not the customary single focal point but several different focal points in one and the same picture.

On 27 August 1792 the architect John Soane bought a house at 12 Lincoln's Inn Fields in central London. The site was well chosen, close to the big construction project he was working on, namely the new Bank of England building. Soane's first impulse was to rebuild the house he had bought, but in the end he decided to pull it down and build a new one. The new house took eighteen months to complete and Soane and his family moved into it in 1794.

Fifteen years earlier he had made the obligatory Grand Tour to Rome, returning to London with his impressions of Piranesi and with a large collection of antique fragments. In Lincoln's Inn Fields, in what was to be his final home, he continued his journey into the labyrinth of history, and here he was to create his own "imaginary prison", inundated with shards of archaeology.

With the passing of time, Soane's collection of books, paintings and sculptures became so large that lack of storage of space was a major problem. The architect toyed with the idea of extending his own house into the backyard of the house next door, No. 13. Three sketches, dated 11 June 1808, show a scheme for a toplit "pilaster room" and delimited "catacomb" galleries in the basement. Later that month John Soane dined with his neighbour and put forward the proposal, which his host unexpectedly agreed to. So behind No. 13 Soane built the part of his home which came to be called "the Dome" and which became his private museum. Soon after its completion, every available space had been covered over with antique fragments and plaster casts.

Entering through the doorway of Soane's house is like stepping into an enchanted world, with its bafflingly intricate weave of rooms, narrow corridors, staircases, unexpected changes of floor level, skylights, openings and mirrors – more than ninety of them in one room. A dreamlike world that has neither beginning nor end. In the museum Soane built in the backyard, classical remains jostle with Gothic fragments and neo-classical details.

The house at No. 13 was bigger than Soane's, and in 1812 he persuaded his neighbour to swap. In 1823 Soane purchased the neighbouring property on the east side, No. 14, and promptly demolished the stables at the rear of it to make room for "the Picture Room" and "Monk's Parlour". During the years that followed, until his death in 1837, alterations, on a greater or lesser scale, were continuously in progress.

Example 2:

"In the wildest and most dramatic part of Capri, in the part which faces south and east, where the island loses its human qualities and turns wrathful, where Nature reveals itself with cruel strength, there is a promontory with an unusual purity of line, a stony claw cast into the sea. No other place in Italy has such a broad horizon and such depth of feeling [...] There was no house there. I was to be the first to build in the midst of this natural scene."

It was on a visit to Capri in December 1937 that the Italian author Curzio Malaparte decided to build himself a house on the island itself. A few months later he bought a plot of land in the southeast of Capri, a wind-swept cliff on the very tip of Punta Masullo commanding a fantastic view of the Mediterranean. He got in touch with the architect Adalberto Libera, one of the leading modernist architects in Rome, commissioning him to design the house. Later that year Libera produced a preliminary draft. The enormous importance attached by Malaparte to his house finally led to a conflict between him and Libera. In 1940 Libera tried to resign the commission, and two years later, when the magazine *Stile* carried an article about his work, Villa Malaparte was not mentioned. Nor does Libera make reference in any of his own writings to the house, which now ranks among his foremost achievements. It is unclear who finally designed the house – Malaparte himself, the local builder Amitrano, Libera, or a combination of all three.

Curzio Malaparte had several names for his house: "*Kase matte*" (casemate or bunker), "*Casa matta*" (madhouse), or "*Casa come me*" (house like me). Malaparte wanted to make the house an architectural portrait of his own composite personality, and the house, as his various names for it suggest, gives rise to a variety of partly conflicting associations, often with a feeling of repugnance and insecurity. Subtle distortions of the shape, structure and floor plan of the house challenge values such as beauty and truth without rejecting them out of hand. Villa Malaparte presents an unusually dramatic contrast between the building and its natural surroundings. It is as though the house had sprung straight out of the rock and then been truncated horizontally at a suitable height. Seen from a distance it resembles a deserted bunker or a ship run aground up on the cliff, while at close quarters it presents striking resemblances to Capri's traditional local architecture. The same kind of duality, with several contradictory languages being spoken at once, permeates the whole structure of the house. The flat roof doubles as a large terrace, like a platform reposing amid the wild natural surroundings. Access to it is gained by the stepped termination on the landward side of the house, and this is where Malaparte took his daily dozen on a bicycle.

The most remarkable interior is the central hall of the *piano nobile*. This is a long, narrow room with two symmetrically positioned windows at each end of the side walls. The furniture in this room is rustic in character and the stone floor puts one in mind of an outdoor terrace. The four huge rectangular windows frame the landscape outside, making it a part of the room's own architecture, but in a way which is both restrained and controlled. The open fireplace is backed with fire-proof Jena glass, enabling one to look through the fire at the water outside.

In his autobiographical novel *La Pelle* (The Skin), Malaparte describes showing a guest round. When the guest is about to leave he asks his host whether he bought the house as it was or designed and built it himself. Malaparte replied that he had bought it as it stood.

And with a sweeping gesture out towards the vertical Mediterranean cliff, the three huge tips of Faraglioni, the Sorrento peninsula, the Siren Islands (Isole de Galli), the distant Amalfi coastline and the glittering beaches of Paestum, Malaparte turned to his guest and said: "I designed the landscape."

Example 3:

Three hours' drive along a straight road from El Paso brings us to Marfa, in the eastern part of Texas. A sign on the outskirts informs us that the place has 2,466 inhabitants, which can hardly be true any longer. The main street is lined by a few shops and Mexican restaurants, but many of the buildings are derelict and boarded up. The town was originally sited here at the intersection of two highways. The old Southern Pacific railway runs parallel to one of them, with endless freight trains thundering by once every hour. The film "Giant" (starring James Dean) was shot in this area in 1956, putting Marfa into a sort of momentary limelight.

At the end of 1946 the American sculptor Donald Judd travelled by bus from Fort McClean in Alabama to Los Angeles and from there to San Francisco, to embark for Korea on military service. It was his first sighting of the southern West, and he telegraphed home:

DEAR MOM. VAN HORN TEXAS. 1260 POPULATION.
NICE TOWN. BEAUTIFUL COUNTRY. MOUNTAINS.
LOVE DON. 1946 17 DEC 17.45.

In 1971 Judd returned to the area, looking for a place to live and to realise an idea of permanent installations of art. Out of growing disgust with the art world and with constantly recurring disappointment over the wrong lighting or wrong room for his own exhibitions was born the idea of permanent installations. He found an abandoned, dilapidated army camp, Fort D. A. Russell, which, with assistance from the Dia Art Foundation, he purchased and began doing up. In 1986 it became a foundation in its own right, the Chinati Foundation, named after a nearby mountain. Since Judd died, in 1994, the place has been run by the foundation, in keeping with his intentions.

In two artillery sheds on the campus Donald Judd installed a work of his own consisting of a hundred rolled aluminium cubes. On the prairie outside, a line of fifteen concrete sculpture groups stretches for a kilometre. In Marfa itself, works by John Chamberlain were installed in an old World War I aircraft hangar.

"The Marfa place was meant to be constructive. The works of art were to be installed permanently, which they will now be in a room that was adapted to suit them. Most of the works were made for the pre-existing buildings, which were decayed. New buildings would have been better. But by altering the old buildings I have transformed them into architecture."

Donald Judd was himself the architect of the Marfa alterations. His architecture, which consists mainly of additions to the existing buildings in the form of new window apertures, new doors or roofs, is a remarkable balancing act between a kind of awkwardness and a strict timelessness. The buildings have undergone a purge that has rid them of everything unnecessary. The architecture does not offer any sensations or visual surprises. Donald Judd was no architect and his working approach is reminiscent more of an exclusive hobby than of a professional activity. Perhaps it is this very distance that has made the result so fascinating. A derelict army camp which has taken on a new lease of life on the borderline between art and architecture.

Edgar Degas. Nude study for the dressed dancer, c. 1921 and Small dancer of fourteen years, c. 1921. Printed by permission of Museu de Arte de São Paulo.

Wheelchair

By Fredrik Nilsson
Architect, researcher and critic, Sweden

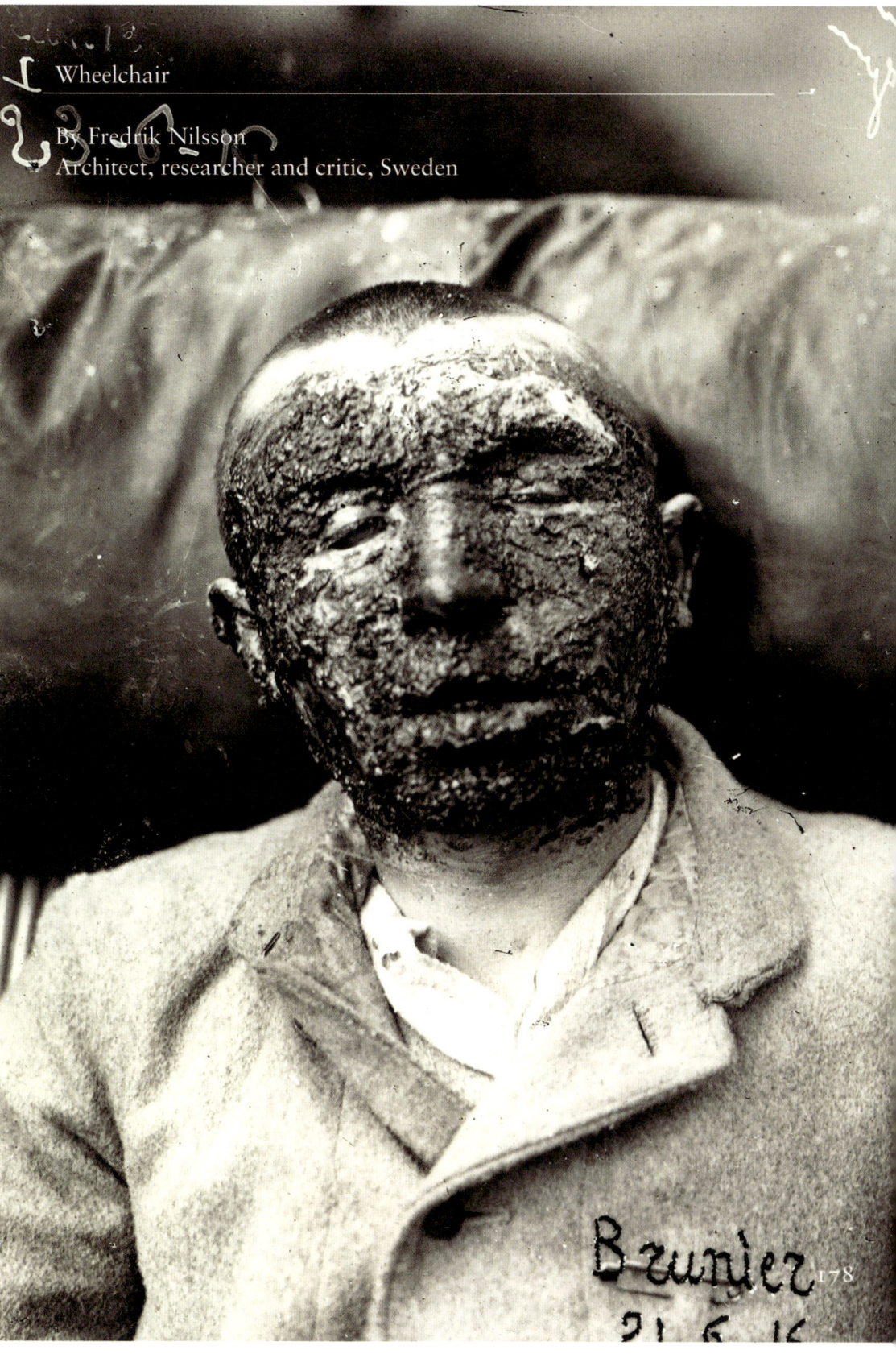

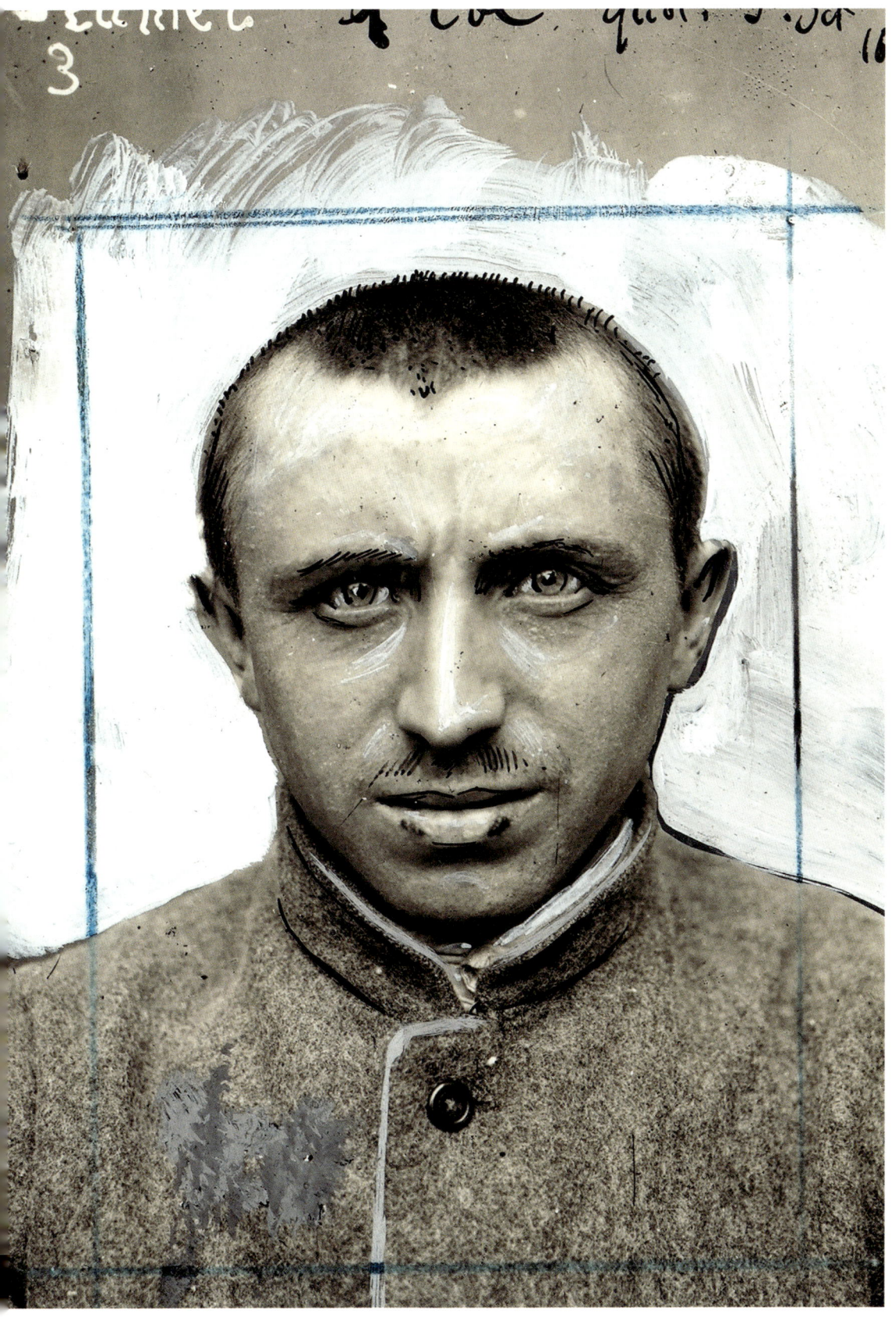

The concept of "wheelchair" can be, and is often, seen as a limiting factor for contemporary architecture; a practical factor imposed by societal norms which reduce or make it harder to fulfil the "higher" ambitions of architecture. But in the notions of wheelchair several important aspects of architecture converge. In what at first may appear to be seemingly simple and almost technical requirements, different perspectives and questions of wider importance condense and connect lines of thought which take us in different directions.

A wheelchair must primarily be seen as something which is connected to notions of "accessibility". It thereby highlights the openness and availability of space and buildings, and increases the opportunities for different people to stay in, use and experience our built environments and cities. Accessibility is, of course, a crucial factor when dealing with "public space", which gives the concept deep political and democratic dimensions. The notion of accessibility is, however, a broad concept in itself. On the one hand it evokes practical and technical solutions which make space readable and accessible for all people – including children, elderly people, as well as people who are temporarily sick or who have disabilities involving the use of wheelchairs; on the other hand accessibility is associated with spatial configuration and the structural organisation of spaces, their hierarchical order and the inherent capacity of architecture to support and create power relations in ways involving the exclusion or inclusion of different groups. The handling of wheelchairs in contemporary architecture thus opens up a broader field of problems, demanding awareness of a wide set of questions, solutions and theoretical perspectives.

The wheelchair can also be strongly associated with notions of the "bodily experience" of space. It is obvious that we experience space with our whole body; we hear sounds, smell scents, and feel the body's contact with the floor and surfaces, often led by the privileged faculty of vision, all of which participate in forming our experiences of spaces and direct our reading and use of them. Movement and transfer through space are important for the bodily and architectural experience, where the position of the body in space and the physical changes of the spatial materiality, involving inclinations, heights, and openings for light or lines of sight etc., yield acceleration, retardation, resistance, and directions. Different spatial experiences of architecture and urban space are generated, depending on whether we sit, stand, or move through space. In a wheelchair you both sit and can be in motion, the body is in close connection to the means of motion. This is like moving in a car, except that one can move through interiors like a cathedral as well, without being restricted to roads and exterior spaces, and where one's eyes are at a different altitude than when standing or walking, which afford different bodily architectural experiences. Exploring and taking advantage of these other experiences is a challenge and an opportunity for architectural development.

The wheelchair is also closely connected to notions of "technology" in architecture. It focuses on the ways in which technology can be an extension of our bodies or how it can expand spatial possibilities and notions. A wheelchair is, like other technological devices, a prosthesis extending the capacity of our bodies and minds. Architecture has always been forced to adapt to new technical means resulting in modified physical, as well as mental, fields of action. Different architectural devices are also contributing to these altered fields of action by changing our notions and perspectives. New technologies influence the way in which we use space, our notions of architecture, our body image and the we have of our position in spatial and organisational contexts. Ramps, elevators, escalators, phase shifting materials, digital screens and communicational tools are devices that have provided new opportunities in contemporary architecture. The technological device known as a wheelchair is a way of improving particular lives in certain ways, which have consequences as well as provide opportunities for the development of architecture. We have to be open-minded and seek out the architectural potentials of both old and new – digital as well as analogue – technologies.

Experience in the profession and artistry of architecture shows that one should not perceive the conditions for contemporary architecture only in terms of constraints, but as a source of inspiration and as an opportunity to consider the task and problem from another perspective. Greater focus on the architectural significance of concepts like "wheelchair" may not only facilitate the life of people with handicaps, but also provide new ways of staging architectural adventures, perceiving technological opportunities, creating accessible spaces, and generating bodily and artistic experiences to the benefit of us all.

Société du Petit Parisien, Dupuy et Cie. The soldier Brunier before his recovery, June 21 and October 7, 1916. Printed by courtesy of Alinari Archives, Florence.

Why

By Orhan Pamuk
Novelist, Turkey and USA

I would stand in awe before the ninety-five-year-old building: Like so many from that era, it was unpainted and had lost plaster here and there, and its dark and dirty surface had the air of some sort of frightening skin disease. The signs of age, neglect, and fatigue were what struck me first. But when I began to notice its little friezes, its witty leaves and trees, and its asymmetrical Art Deco designs, I forgot its sickly appearance, thinking instead of the happy, easy life this building had once enjoyed. I saw many cracks and holes in its rainspouts, its weatherboard, its friezes, and its eaves. Inspecting the several stories, including the shop on the ground floor, I could see that, like most buildings built a hundred years ago, it had originally been a four-story construction, the top two stories having been added twenty years ago. There were no friezes, no thick weatherboarding over the windows, and no fine handiwork on the facade. Sometimes these floors would not even be of the same height as those below, nor would their windows be aligned in the same way. Most of these floors had been added very hastily, profiting from home improvement drives, loopholes in the law, and corrupt mayors turning a blind eye. Perhaps at first sight they had looked modern and clean next to the building's original century-old facade; twenty years later, their interiors seemed older and more dilapidated than those of the floors below.

When I would look up at the little bay windows, the traditional Istanbul architect's signature, hanging out over the street by three feet – my eye would settle on a flowerpot or a child peering out at me. My mind would automatically calculate that this building sat on a plot of about eight hundred and fifty square feet, work out how much usable space there was, and try to figure out whether or not it suited my needs. I was not looking for a building to turn into a home; I had begun to search Istanbul's oldest neighborhoods – streets going back two thousand years: the back streets of Galata, Beyoğlu, and Cihangir, where Greeks and Armenians had once lived and, before them, the Genoese – for a stranger purpose. I needed this house for a book and a museum.

As I was gazing at the building from across the street, the grocer from the shop behind me came outside to tell me about the building – what condition it was in, how old it was, and who owned it – making it clear to me that the owner had engaged him to act on his behalf, if only as his eyes and ears.

"Would it be possible for me to go inside?" I asked, somewhat anxiously, not wishing to enter a strange house without the permission of those living in it.

"Go right in, brother, go right in and take a look, don't worry!" bellowed the worldly grocer. Though it was a hot summer day, the entrance hall was spacious and extraordinarily cool (they don't make these beautiful high-ceilinged entrance halls anymore, not even in apartment buildings in the wealthiest areas), and I could no longer hear the cries of the children in the shabby sheets outside or the noise from the plastics and machine shops opposite, only a few paces away, and all this reminded me that the houses in this area had been built with a very different sort of life in mind. I went up to the second floor, and then to the third, and with the encouragement of the curious grocer behind me, I entered whatever door, whatever apartment, I pleased. The people living here might not all be from the same family, but they came from the same Anatolian village and they kept their doors unlocked. As I wandered through these apartments, I greedily registered everything I saw, like a camera making a silent film.

Outside an apartment that led out to the entrance hall, I saw a woman dozing in an old bed pushed next to the wall. Before she could come out of her daze to look at me closely, I had gone into the adjoining room (there was no corridor), where I found four children between the ages of five and eight squeezed together on a little divan in front of a colour television set. No one lifted a head to look at me; the little toes of their bare feet, which were dangling over the side of the high divan, were twitching to the rhythms of the adventure film they were watching.

When I wandered into the next room in this crowded house that was as quiet as the midday heat, I met a woman who at once reminded me of the days when I'd had to supply my name, rank, and serial number: "Who are you?" asked this frowning mother, in her hand a huge teapot. As the grocer behind me explained the situation, I noticed that the room in which the woman was working was not a proper kitchen; the only access to this narrow space was through a room in which an elderly man was resting in his underpants, and of course I understood that the present configuration was not the original plan for this building. I tried to imagine what this floor had once looked like. I formed a sense of the underpants man's room in its entirety, staring at the walls, which, like all the others I had seen (except in the grocery) were flaking paint and plaster and a severe embarrassment.

With the help of neighborhood gossips and with eager guidance from the grocer, who had by now transformed from a helpful go-between into a real estate agent, as well as real agents working on commission, I spent the next month visiting hundreds of old apartments in that area – in a street where all the residents were Kurds from Tunceli, the Roma neighborhood in Galata, where all the women and children sat on the stoop to watch the passersby, or the alley where bored old ladies would shout down from their windows, "Why doesn't he come up and look at this place too?" I saw half-collapsed kitchens, old sitting rooms haphazardly divided in two, staircases whose steps had been worn away; rooms with broken wooden floorboards concealed under carpets; storerooms, machine shops, restaurants, and old luxury apartments with fine plaster work on their walls and ceilings, now being used as chandelier shops; empty buildings rotting away with no owners, or else owners who had emigrated or were locked in a property dispute; rooms with little children crammed in as tightly as objects in a cupboard; cool ground floors whose damp walls smelled of mold; basements in which someone had carefully stowed wood, gathered from underneath trees and from rubbish bins and the city's back streets, along with pieces of iron and all variety of rubbish; staircases in which no step was the same height as any other; leaky ceilings; buildings in which the lifts didn't work and the lights didn't work either; women in head scarves who watched through cracks in their doors as I walked past them on the stairs and past people sleeping in their beds; balconies where they'd hung their washing, walls that said NO LITTERING! and children playing in courtyards; and enormous wardrobes that all resembled one another and dwarfed everything else in the bedroom.

If I hadn't visited so many houses one after the other, I would never have seen so clearly the two essential things that people did in their homes: (1) Stretch out in a chair or on a divan, a sofa, a cushioned bench, or a bed and doze, and (2) watch television all the hours of the day. Most of the time they did both at the same time, while also smoking and drinking tea. In areas of the city where property values were about the same, there was much too much space given over to stairs; I saw no houses that departed from this design. After seeing how much room was taken up by staircases in buildings with barely fifteen or twenty feet of frontage and no rooms in the back, I tried to forget the facades, buildings, and streets of the city and conjure up hundreds of thousands of staircases and stairwells; having done so, I came to see the divided properties of Istanbul as a forest of secret stairways.

At the end of my travels, what impressed me most was to see how these buildings, which despite their facades were small and humble dwellings made a hundred years ago for the city's Greek and Levantine populations by Armenian architects and contractors, were being used in ways so amazingly different from the ways that their builders could have hoped for or conceived. I had learned one thing from my years studying architecture: Buildings take the shape of their architects' and buyers' dreams. After the Greeks, Armenians, and Levantines who had dreamed up these buildings were forced to leave them in the early years of the last century, they came to reflect the imaginations of the succeeding occupants. I am not talking here about an active imagination shaping these buildings and streets to give the city a certain look. I am talking of the passive imagination of people who came from faraway places to streets and buildings already looking a certain way, who then changed their dreams to adapt to it.

I can liken this sort of imagination to that of a child who conjures up visions from the shadows on the walls before he goes to sleep in a dark room in the middle of the night. If he is sleeping in a strange and frightening room, he can make it bearable by imagining the familiar. If he is in a clean room he knows well, a room where he feels secure, he can build himself a dream world by likening the shadows to frightening creatures from legends. In both instances, his imagination is working with the fragmented and haphazard material at hand to create dreams that fit in with the place where the child happens to be. So the imagination in question is not in service to a person who is creating new worlds on a blank sheet of paper, it is in service to someone who is trying to fit in with a world already made. The waves of migration that Istanbul saw over the past century, the shifting of industries from one neighborhood to another, the emergence of a new Turkish bourgeoisie, the dreams of Westernization that had prompted some people to abandon these buildings and dilapidated rooms, to be replaced by others from elsewhere – everywhere you looked in Istanbul, you saw signs of that second, accommodating, imagination. The people who had built these partitions, who had turned stairwells and bay windows into kitchens and entrance halls into storerooms or waiting rooms, who had created living space by putting beds and wardrobes in the most unexpected places, who had bricked up walls and windows or put new windows and doors into walls or knocked holes through them, who had equipped all the stoves in these buildings with pipes that snaked across every wall and ceiling – who had taken all these measures to turn these places into home – these people were utterly foreign to the intentions of the architects who had conceived these houses a century earlier.

It is not by chance that I speak of blank sheets of paper. I studied architecture at Istanbul Technical University for about three years, but I did not graduate to become an architect. I now think that this had to do with the ostentatious modernist dreams I set down on those blank sheets. All I knew at the time was that I did not want to become an architect – or a painter, as I had dreamed for many years. I abandoned the great empty architectural drawing sheets that thrilled and frightened me, making my head spin, and instead sat down to stare at the blank writing paper that thrilled and frightened me just as much. That's where I've been sitting for twenty-five years now. As a book takes shape in my mind, I believe myself to be at the beginning of everything; I believe that the world will conform to my ideas – just as I did when I dreamed up buildings as an architectural student.

So let's ask the question that I heard quite a lot twenty-five years ago and that I still ask myself from time to time: Why didn't I become an architect? Answer: Because I thought the sheets of paper on which I was to pour my dreams were blank. But after twenty-five years of writing, I have come to understand that those pages are never blank. I know very well now that when I sit down at my table, I am sitting with tradition and with those who refuse absolutely to bow to rules or to history; I am sitting with things born of coincidence and disorder, darkness, fear, and dirt, with the past and its ghosts, and all the things that officialdom and our language wish to forget; I am sitting with fear and with the dreams to which fear gives rise. To bring all these things to the page, I had to write novels that drew from the past, and all the things that the Westernizers and the modern Republic wished to forget, but that embraced the future and the imagination at the same time. Had I thought, at the age of twenty, that I could do the same with architecture, I might well have become an architect. But in those days I was a resolute modernist who wished to escape from the burden, the filth, and the ghost-ridden twilight that was history – and what's more, I was an optimistic Westernizer, certain that all was going to plan. As for the peoples of the city in which I lived who conformed to no rules with their complex communities and their histories – they did not figure in my dreams: I saw them instead as obstacles, there to keep my dreams from being realized. I understood at once that they would never let me make the sorts of buildings I wanted in those streets. But they would not object if I shut myself up in my own house and wrote about them.

It took me eight years to publish my first book. Throughout this time, and especially at the points when I had lost hope that anyone would ever publish me, I had a recurring dream: I am an architecture student, and I am in an architectural design class, planning a building, but there is very little time left before I have to hand my design in. I am sitting at a table, putting everything I have into my work, surrounded by half-finished sketches and rolls of paper and, on all sides, inkstains are opening up like poison flowers. As I labour on, ideas come to me that are even more brilliant than the ones I had before, but despite my feverish efforts the fearsome deadline is fast approaching, and I know full well that I have no more chance of realizing this great new idea than I have of finishing the building on my sheet of paper. It is my fault that I cannot finish my project in the time I have left, my fault entirely. As I conjure up visions of ever greater intensity, I am so racked by guilt that the pain wakes me up.

The first thing to say about the fear that gave rise to this dream is that it is the fear of becoming a writer. Had I become an architect, I would at least have had a proper profession and would at least have been able to earn enough money to enjoy a middle-class life. But when I began to say, somewhat obscurely, that I was going to be a writer and write novels, my family told me I would suffer financial hardship in the years ahead. So in the face of all that guilt and that fearful running out of time, this was a dream that assuaged the pain of my longings. Because when I was studying to be an architect, I was still part of "normal" life. To work this hard, against the clock, and to dream intensely – this would only characterise my life later on, when I was writing novels against no deadlines whatsoever.

In those days, when people asked me why I had not become an architect, I would give the same answer in different words: "Because I didn't want to design apartments!" When I said *apartments*, I meant a way of life as well as a particular approach to architecture. It was during the 1930s that Istanbul's old historic neighborhoods emptied out, as the moneyed classes began to tear down their two- and three-story houses with their spacious gardens, using these and other empty lots for apartment buildings that within sixty years had utterly destroyed the city's old fabric. When I began school in the late 1950s, every child in my class lived in an apartment. In the beginning, the facades mixed a plain Bauhaus modernism with traditionally Turkish bay windows; later on they became poor, uninspired copies of the international style; and because the inheritance law ensured that many of the plots on which one built were very narrow, their interiors were

all identical. Between them were stairwells and narrow ventilation shafts that some called "the darkness" and others "the light"; in the front was the sitting room and in the back, according to the size of the plot and the skill of the architect, were two or three bedrooms. There were long narrow corridors connecting the single front room with the several rooms at the back; these, along the windows looking out onto "the light" and the windows in the stairwell, made all these apartments look terrifyingly alike; and they all smelled of mold, cooking oil, bird droppings, and want. What frightened me most during my years of studying architecture was the prospect of having to design cost-effective apartments on these narrow little plots in accordance with current housing regulations and the tastes of the half-Westernized middle class. In those days, many relatives and acquaintances who complained about dishonorable architects told me that, once I was an architect, they would make sure I could build my own apartments on the empty lots owned by their parents.

By not becoming an architect, I was able to escape this fate. I became a writer, and I have written a great deal about apartments. What I have learned from everything I have written is this: A building's homeliness issues from the dreams of those who live in it. These dreams, like all dreams, are nourished by that building's old, dark, dirty, and disintegrating corners. Just as in some buildings we see facades become more beautiful with age, and interior walls take on a mysterious texture, so too can we see the traces of its journey from a building with no meaning into a home, a construction of dreams. This is how I understand the partitioned rooms, punctured walls, and broken staircases I described earlier. These are things for which an architect can find neither the traces nor the proof: the dreams with which the person who first occupies a new and ordinary building (conceived in a burst of modernizing, Westernizing enthusiasm and made as if it were starting from the beginning) turns it into a home.

When I was walking among the ruins of the earthquake that killed 30,000 people, I felt the presence of this imagination again, and very powerfully – walking among all those fragments of walls, bricks, and concrete, broken windows, slippers, lamp bases, curtains, and carpets: every building, every shelter, new or old, that a person entered, it was his imagination that turned it into a home. Like Dostoyevsky's heroes, who use their imaginations to cling to life even in the most hopeless circumstances, we too know how to turn our buildings into homes, even when life is very hard.

But when these homes are destroyed by an earthquake, we are painfully reminded that they are also buildings. Just after that earthquake that killed 30,000 people, my father told me how he'd found his way out of one apartment house and groped his way through the pitch-dark street to take refuge in another apartment building two hundred yards away. When I asked why he had done so, he said, "Because that building's safe. I made it myself." He meant the family apartment house where I had spent my childhood, the building we once shared with my grandmother, my uncles, and my aunts, and that I have described so often – in so many novels – and if my father took refuge there, I would say it was not because it was a safe building but because it was a home.

The authors

Biographies, Art and photography

The authors

Nicholas Adams is Mary Conover Mellon Professor in the History of Architecture at Vassar College in Poughkeepsie, NY. He is a member of the editorial board of the Italian architectural magazine Casabella and is the author of Skidmore, Owings & Merrill: SOM since 1936 (London: Phaidon, 2007). He has served as editor of the Journal of the Society of Architectural Historians and his essays and reviews have appeared in Architectural Record, Harvard Design Magazine, and Arkitektur. He has been a fellow of the American Academy in Rome and the Institute for Advanced Study, Princeton. He has also taught in the architectural schools at Harvard University, Columbia University, and UCLA.

Mikael Bergquist, architect SAR/MSA, born in 1961. Graduated from KTH, Stockholm and Academy of Fine Arts, Copenhagen 1990. In 1996 he established his studio in Stockholm. Awarded the Östergötland Architectural Prize in 2004. Freelance editor of The Swedish Review of Architecture 1996–2002. Curator and editor of a number of exhibitions and books, the latest Accidentism: Josef Frank, (Birkhäuser, 2005).

Peter Blundell Jones, architect, has been involved in practice, criticism and teaching for most of his professional life, but with an increasing emphasis on architectural history and theory. Professor of Architecture at the University of Sheffield in 1994, where he has remained until now. As a journalist and critic, he has enjoyed a long and close working relationship with The Architectural Review. The books include the revised Hans Scharoun (Phaidon, London, 1995), Dialogues in Time, the story of the Austrian Grazer Schule (Haus der Architektur, Graz, 1998), Hugo Häring: the Organic versus the Geometric (Edition Menges 1999), Günter Behnisch (Birkhäuser 2000), Gunnar Asplund (Phaidon 2006), Modern Architecture through Case Studies 1945–1990 (a second volume, Architectural Press, 2007), and Peter Hübner: Building as a Social Process (Menges 2007).

Marie-Ange Brayer has been director of the Centre Regional Contemporary Art Collection [FRAC, Centre] in Orléans, France since 1996, where the collection is channelled towards the linkage between art and research architecture. She has organized many exhibitions, and conferences, mainly based on this collection both in France and abroad. In 2002, Marie-Ange Brayer and Béatrice Simonot were co-curators of the French pavilion at the 8th International architectural biennale in Venice. She is currently working on a PhD retracing the legal status of the architectural model since the Renaissance.

Jonas Edblad, Architect SAR/MSA born in 1962 in Gothenburg, Sweden. Graduated from Chalmers University of Technology (CTH), Gothenburg in 1991. Employed at Wingårdh Arkitektkontor in 1991. Awarded with the Kasper Salin prize 2001 (Student union, Chalmers University of Technology, Gothenburg) and 2006 (Aranäsgymnasiet, senior high school, Kungsbacka).

Massimiliano Fuksas was born in Rome in 1944, where he graduated in Architecture at "La Sapienza University" in 1969. In 1967, 1989 and 1993 he established practices in Rome, Paris and Vienna respectively and since 2002 he opened a new studio in Frankfurt. From 1998 to 2000 he was Director of the VII Biennale Internazionale di Architettura di Venezia "Less Aesthetics, More Ethics". Visiting Professor at several universities and columnist at the weekly magazine "L'Espresso". Has worked with Doriana O. Mandrelli since 1985.

Elisa Fuksas, born 1981. Graduated from Università di Roma 3, Faculty of Architecture in 2005 and has been working mainly with writing, directing and editing film. Writer for Italian culture magazine "Panorama" and ghost-writer for "L'Espresso".

Catharina Gabrielsson, Swedish architect (KTH 1992) and Ph.D. She has taken part in and/or organized numerous lecture series, seminars, discussions and exhibitions on the subject of art, architecture and urban planning. Chairperson for the Government's Council of Architecture, Form and Design (2004–05). Member of the editorial board of MAMA (Magazine for Modern Architecture). She is one of the founding members of Färgfabriken, Centre of Art and Architecture (Stockholm) and has been responsible for the implementation of numerous public art projects on behalf of the Swedish National Public Art Council.

Ingerid Helsing Almaas, born 1965 in Oslo, is an architect. She was educated at the Architectural Association in London, where she has also taught for a number of years. She has worked as an architect in London and in Oslo, taught and lectured in Scandinavia and abroad and has also practised architecture as a freelance writer and critic for a number of international publications. She is currently editor-in-chief of Arkitektur N, the Norwegian review of architecture.

Hans Ibelings, born in Rotterdam 1963, is an architectural historian. He worked for the Netherlands Architecture Institute in Rotterdam, taught at the EPFL in Lausanne and is the author of several books, including Supermodernism: Architecture in the Age of Globalization. He is editor and publisher of the bimonthly magazine A10 new European architecture, which he founded, together with graphic designer Arjan Groot.

Falk Jaeger, professor, born 1950, studied architecture and history of art. He worked 1983–88 for the Institute of History of Architecture at the Berlin University of Technology. 1993 to 2000 he was appointed Chair of Theory of Architecture at the Dresden University of Technology. 2001 until 2002, he was editor in chief of the German architecture magazine Bauzeitung. Today he is living in Berlin as a freelance critic, editor and curator, working on architecture, theory and history of architecture for major newspapers and architecture magazines, radio and television.

Vittorio Magnago Lampugnani, architect and professor. Born in Rome in 1951. Studied architecture in Rome and in Stuttgart; in 1977 doctorate. Professor of Architecture in Harvard, Frankfurt am Main and Pamplona. Since 1994 Professor for the History of Urban Design at the Swiss Federal Institute of Technology (ETH) in Zurich. The most important projects of his Studio di architettura in Milan include: office building in Block 109, Berlin (1991–96); housing group in Maria Lankowitz near Graz (1995–99); entrance square of the Audi factory in Ingolstadt (1999–2000); urban design planning of Novartis Campus in St. Johann, Basel, (2001 ff.); underground station Mergellina, Naples (2004ff); reshaping of the Danube banks, Regensburg (2004ff). Numerous scholarly architectural publications and exhibitions.

Maria Lantz, born 1962, trained as a photographer at the International Center of Photography in New York and at the University of Gothenburg. Since 1999 appointed to the Royal University College of Fine Arts in Stockholm, where she runs the education program on art and architecture. Editor for Motiv, a magazine on contemporary photography and an active artist, working with subjects such as place, architecture, stories and memories.

Johan Linton is an architect, civil engineer in technical physics and currently working on a Ph.D. in the theory and history of architecture. He runs his own practice as architect and graphic designer and has designed several items of furniture that have commanded great attention. Member of the editorial board of Psykoanalytisk Tid/Skrift (Magazine for psychoanalysis).

Nils-Ole Lund, Danish architect and author, born 1930. Assistant Professor in Architecture at the University of Trondheim, 1953, professor at the new School of Architecture in Aarhus in 1963. Headmaster of the same school 1972–85, and president of the European Union of Schools of Architecture EAAI, 1991–95. Author of numerous books on architecture, most notably Nordisk arkitektur (1991) and Teoriutdannelser i arkitekturen (1970).

Fredrik Nilsson, architect SAR/MSA, PhD, researcher and critic, working at Chalmers School of Architecture and at White Arkitekter. He has taught and lectured widely, and has written on, in particular, contemporary architecture, architectural theory and philosophy with a special interest in the interaction between conceptual, theoretical thinking and practical design work. Nilsson is author and editor of several books and frequently publishes articles, architectural criticism and reviews of books.

Hans Ulrich Obrist was born in Zurich in May 1968. He joined the Serpentine Gallery as co-director of exhibitions and programmes and director of international projects in April 2006. Prior to this he was curator of the Musée d'Art Moderne de la Ville de Paris from 2000, and curator of museum in progress, Vienna, from 1993–2000. He has curated over 150 exhibitions internationally since 1991, including do it, Take Me, I'm Yours (Serpentine Gallery), Cities on the Move, Live/Life, Nuit Blanche, 1st Berlin Biennale,

Manifesta 1, and more recently Uncertain States of America, 1st Moscow Triennale and 2nd Guangzhou Biennale (Canton, China).

Juhani Pallasmaa, born 1936, architect SAFA, Hon. FAIA, professor, has practised architecture since the early 1960s and established Pallasmaa Architects in 1983. He has been active in urban planning, architectural exhibition, product and graphic design, taught and lectured widely in Europe, North and South America, Africa and Asia, and published nineteen books and numerous essays on the philosophies of architecture and art in thirty languages. He has held positions including Professor and Dean at the Helsinki University of Technology (1991–97), Director of the Museum of Finnish Architecture (1978–83), Rector of the Institute of Industrial Arts (1970–71), and visiting professorships at several universities in the USA.

Henrietta Palmer, architect SAR/MSA, educated at Royal Institute of Technology and at the Laboratory of Urbanism of Cities, Barcelona. She is a professor in architecture at the Royal University College of Fine Arts, running a multi-disciplinary postgraduate education programme, resources, focusing on architecture and urban planning from a sustainable perspective. 2001 she took part in the planning of the conference Art+Architecture, Monument +Propaganda, Stockholm. Writer, critic and jury member, most recently in Europan 9.

Orhan Pamuk, Turkish novelist, born in Istanbul 1952. Studied architecture for three years at the Istanbul Technical University, but left school to become a full-time writer. Author of numerous books on Turkey's double identity between east and west, where his own urban background in a bourgeois family has a profound role. His books have been translated into more than thirty languages and he has been awarded some of the world's most distinguished prizes, including the Nobel Prize for Literature 2006. "Why Didn't I Become an Architect" has previously been published in the collection "The Other Colours".

Joseph Rykwert is Paul Philippe Cret Professor of Architecture Emeritus at the University of Pennsylvania. He was born in Warsaw and emigrated to England in 1939. Following his architectural studies at the Bartlett School of Architecture and the Architectural Association, he taught at Hammersmith School of Arts & Crafts and the Hochschule für Gestaltung, Ulm before becoming Librarian and Tutor at the Royal College of Art in London. In 1967 he became Professor of Art at the newly created University of Essex where he remained until 1981 when he was first Slade Professor in the Fine Arts at the University of Cambridge and then Reader in Architecture. His publications include: The Golden House (1947), The Idea of a Town (1963), On Adam's House in Paradise (1972), The First Moderns (1980), The Necessity of Artifice (1982), The Brothers Adam (1984), a new translation of Alberti's architecture treatise, On the Art of Building in Ten Books (1989, with Robert Tavernor and Neil Leach), The Dancing Column (1996) and The Seduction of Place (2000).

Jaime Salazar Rückauer, Architect. Born 1964 in Bilbao (Spain), he studied architecture at the Universitat Politecnica de Catalunya in Barcelona. Between 1991 and 1999 he worked as editor at the architecture magazine Quaderns from the Catalan chamber of architects, with Manuel Gausa as editor-in-chief. He later worked as editor for architecture at the editorial house Actar in Barcelona between 1996 and 2002 and published books including Singe Family Housing. The Private Domain (1999), MVRDV at VPRO (1998) and the boogazine Verb (2000). Since 2002 he has lived and worked in Bochum (Germany).

Irénée Scalbert is an architecture critic based in London. He has contributed articles and essays to most European magazines on a wide range of historical and contemporary issues. He is the author of A Right to Difference: The Architecture of Jean Renaudie (2004). He has taught at the Architectural Association for many years and is a member of the editorial board of AA Files. He was Visiting Design Critic in 2006 and 2007 at the Graduate School of Design, Harvard. In addition to his teaching, he is a regular guest lecturer.

Robert Schäfer, born 1954, studied landscape planning in Berlin and journalism in Stuttgart-Hohenheim. In 1984 he joined Garten+Landschaft, one of the leading landscape architecture journals and also founded Topos, European Landscape Magazine in 1992. After a complete relaunch, Topos went global in 2005 with the new subtitle "The International Review of Landscape Architecture and Urban Design".

Denise Scott Brown. As an architect, planner, urban designer, theorist, writer and educator, Scott Brown

supports a broadening of architecture to include ideas on multiculturalism, social concern and activism, Pop Art, popular culture, the everyday landscape; symbolism, iconography and context. As a principal in Venturi, Scott Brown and Associates of Philadelphia, she takes an urban approach to the firm's institutional architecture and is in charge of its planning and urban design. Her projects have included campus plans and building complexes for Dartmouth College and the Universities of Pennsylvania and Michigan.

Axel Sowa, born 1966 in Essen, Germany, studied architecture in Berlin and Paris. He worked in the office of Bruno Rollet in Paris. In 1995, he received a grant form the Carl-Duisberg-Gesellschaft in Cologne that enabled him to study and practise architecture in Kyoto, Japan. Axel Sowa contributed to various magazines before he started to work permanently with L'Architecture d'Aujourd'hui in 1998. Since January 2000 he has been the magazine's editor-in-chief. In parallel to his editorial work, Axel Sowa has been teaching history and theory of architecture at the University of Applied Sciences in Saarbrücken, Germany.

Sverker Sörlin is Professor of Environmental History in the Division of History of Science and Technology at the Royal Institute of Technology, Stockholm. He has held visiting positions at the University of California, Berkeley (1993), the University of Cambridge (2004–05), and the University of Oslo (2006). Sörlin has published widely on the history of the concept of nature and on landscape history in journals such as Environmental History, Worldviews, Kursbuch, and in the exhibition catalogue for Documenta 11 (2002). He wrote the article on "Nature" for Dictionary of the History of Science (London, 2000) and his book on nature in the history of ideas, The Nature Contract (Naturkontraktet, 1991, in Swedish), was shortlisted for the August [for Strindberg] Prize and has remained in print.

Carsten Thau, born 1947, Professor of Architectural Theory and History at the Royal Danish Academy of Fine Arts, School of Architecture, former Associate Professor at The School of Architecture in Aarhus and Associate Professor in Cultural Studies at the Department of Comparative Literature and Modern Culture at the University of Copenhagen. Studied philosophy in Frankfurt am Main. Critic for the Danish Daily Information 1980–90. Has written articles and books about architecture, design, urbanistics, and film. His publications include a book about the Danish designer and architect Arne Jacobsen (with Kjeld Vindum). His most recent book is Filosofi og Arkitektur, Copenhagen 2006.

Marc Treib is Professor Emeritus of Architecture at the University of California, Berkeley, a practicing designer, and a frequent contributor to architecture, landscape and design journals. He has held Fulbright, Guggenheim, and Japan Foundation fellowships, as well as an advanced design fellowship at the American Academy in Rome. Recent publications include: Noguchi in Paris: The Unesco Garden (2003), Thomas Church, Landscape Architect: Designing a Modern California Landscape (2004), and The Donnell and Eckbo Gardens: Modern Californian Masterworks (2005) (all William Stout Publishers), and Settings and Stray Paths: Writings on Landscape Architecture (2005, Routledge).

Wilfried Wang is the O'Neil Ford Centennial Professor in Architecture at the University of Texas at Austin and founder of the Berlin practice of Hoidn Wang Partner. Wang studied architecture in London. He was co-editor of 9H Magazine and co-director of the 9H Gallery. He was the director of the German Architecture Museum (1995–2000). Wang is the author of various monographs and topographs on the architecture of the twentieth century. He is the chairman of the Erich-Schelling Foundation, an honorary member of the Federation of German Architects (BDA) and of the Royal Academy of Fine Arts in Stockholm.

Janet Ward, Associate Professor of History at the University of Nevada Las Vegas, is an interdisciplinary scholar of German and comparative urban studies, European cultural history, modernism, visual culture, memory studies, architectural theory, and the German twentieth century, with specific focus on the Weimar and Nazi eras. Janet Ward's publications include Weimar Surfaces: Urban Visual Culture in 1920s Germany (University of California Press, 2001); German Studies in the Post-Holocaust Age: The Politics of Memory, Identity, and Ethnicity (University of Colorado Press, 2000, co-edited with Adrian Del Caro); and Agonistics: Arenas of Creative Contest (State University of New York Press, 1997, co-edited with Elizabeth Sauer).

The editors

Gert Wingårdh, architect and professor, born 1951. After studying history and theory of art he quickly settled on architecture. Soon after graduation in 1975 he started his own practice. It has grown steadily, and Wingårdh Arkitektkontor AB today is one of the largest architect practices in Sweden, with about 120 employees and with projects in several continents. Their artistic aspirations have earned it numerous accolades. Parallel to his architectural practice, Gert Wingårdh has also taken part in the public discussion of architectural issues and has been actively involved in teaching, most recently as Artistic Professor at the School of Architecture at Chalmers University of Technology.

Rasmus Wærn, architect and Ph.D. in history of architecture, born 1961. Connected to Wingårdh Architects and to the Royal Institute of Technology in Stockholm, Sweden. Author and collaborator in numerous books and articles on Swedish architecture, such as Guide to the Architecture of Sweden (2001, Arkitektur Förlag) and Gert Wingårdh, Architect (2001, Birkhäuser Verlag). Curator of the exhibition Architektur im 20. Jahrhundert: Schweden at the German Museum of Architecture. An editor of the Swedish Review of Architecture 1996–2004. Chairman of the Swedish Alvar Aalto Society.

Art and photography

Werner Blaser, 12
Bill Viola, 16
Giorgio De Chirico, 22
Photographer unknown, 32
Philip Johnson, 52
Francesco Clemente, 60–61
Edward R. Tufte, 64
Georg Stubbs, 76
Giuseppe Sammartino, 88
Gaëtan Gatian de Clérambault, 94–95
Adolf Wissel, 107
Marcus Larsson, 110
Pöyry Energy AG, 122
Esko Männikkö, 130–131
Musées Royaux d'Art et d'Histoire, 142
Andreas Gursky, 150–151
Andres Serrano, 158–159
Scanpix/Corbis, 160
Edgar Degas, 170–171
Société du Petit Parisien, 178–179
Bruce Chatwin, 189

Editors: Gert Wingårdh and Rasmus Wærn
Editorial advisors: Mikael Bergquist and Henrietta Palmer
Production: Henrik Nygren Design AB
Art and photography consultant: Björn Springfeldt
Translations: Roger Tanner and Maureen Freely

Printing and binding: Fälth & Hässler, Värnamo, Sweden 2007
Letterpress printing: Norrbacka Tryckeri
Printed on acid-free paper produced from chlorine-free pulp. TCF ∞
Paper: Lessebo Design Natural 150 gsm from Vida Papers

Text by Orhan Pamuk printed by permission of The Wylie Agency, London.
Original title *Why Didn't I Become an Architect*. Thanks to Dilek Gür

Library of Congress Control Number: 2007937774

Any claims for image copyrights note cleared shall be addressed to wingardhs@wingardhs.se

Bibliographic information published by the German National Library
The German National Library lists this publication in the Deutsche Nationalbibliografie; detailed bibliographic data are available on the Internet at http://dnb.d-nb.de.

This work is subject to copyright. All rights are reserved, whether the whole or part of the material is concerned, specifically the rights of translation, reprinting, re-use of illustrations, recitation, broadcasting, reproduction on microfilms or in other ways, and storage in data bases.
For any kind of use permission of the copyright owner must be obtained.

© 2008 Wingårdh Arkitektkontor AB

© 2008 Birkhäuser Verlag AG
Basel · Boston · Berlin
P. O. Box 133, CH-4010 Basel, Switzerland
Part of Springer Science+Business Media

ISBN-13: 978-3-7643-8645-0

Contents

Introduction, 2

Crucial Words:
Architects, 10
Atmosphere, 14
Body, 18
City Branding, 26
Competitions, 30
Computer, 36
Concept, 40
Corporate, 46
Desire, 56
Doers, 62
Europe, 66
Everyday, 72
Experiment, 78
Formalism, 84
Future, 90
Globalization, 98
Humanism, 104
Landscape, 110
Memory, 114
Modernity, 118
Nature, 122
Nordic, 128
Organic, 134
Ornament, 138
Photography, 146
Slit, 154
Technology, 160
Tradition, 164
Transformation, 170
Wheelchair, 178
Why, 182

Biographies, 197
Art and photography, 207